# Setting up & Running a
# Complementary Health Practice

*Other related titles published by How To Books*

**Your Own Business**
*The complete guide to succeeding with a small business*

**Book-keeping & Accounting for the Small Business**
*How to keep the books and maintain financial control over your business*

**Starting Your Own Business**
*How to plan, build and manage a successful enterprise*

**The Ultimate Business Plan**
*Secure financial backing and support for a successful business*

**howto**books

Please send for a free copy of the latest catalogue:

How To Books
3 Newtec Place, Magdalen Road,
Oxford OX4 1RE, United Kingdom
email: info@howtobooks.co.uk
http://www.howtobooks.co.uk

# Setting up & Running a Complementary Health Practice

## Patricia Bishop

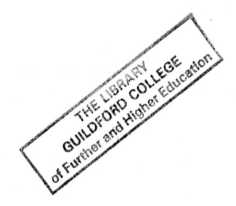

**howto**books

Dedicated to the memory of my father, Harry, for his belief in me

Published by How To Books Ltd
3 Newtec Place, Magdalen Road
Oxford OX4 1RE, United Kingdom
Tel: (01865) 793806 Fax: (01865) 248780
info@howtobooks.co.uk
www.howtobooks.co.uk

First published 2004

British Library Cataloguing in Publication Data.
A catalogue record for this book is available from the British Library.

Edited by Diana Brueton
Cover design by Baseline Arts Ltd, Oxford
Produced for How To Books by Deer Park Productions
Typeset by PDQ Typesetting, Newcastle-under-Lyme, Staffs.
Printed and bound in Great Britain by Bell & Bain Ltd, Glasgow

NOTE: The material contained in this book is set out in good faith for general
guidance and no liability can be accepted for loss or expense incurred as a result of
relying in particular circumstances on statements made in the book. Laws and
regulations are complex and liable to change, and readers should check the current
position with the relevant authorities before making personal arrangements.

# Contents

# A Brief Word Before You Start

*Starting up – keep it simple*

The good news, for most complementary therapists, is that the start-up costs for setting up a complementary health practice can be kept very low. Many therapists have built up thriving practices whilst operating out of a spare room at home, taking over a regular morning or afternoon slot at a nearby clinic or practice, or sharing rooms with a local colleague or friend. If you keep whatever equipment you require to a minimum and realistically prioritise what is *essential* for your particular therapy, then you may be pleasantly surprised at how cheaply and easily you can set up in practice.

If you are just starting out, then building up a practice does take time. All those comments you've heard from well-meaning friends and family do have some basis in truth. Complementary therapy practices take as long as any other business to establish, and you should, therefore, allow a full two years to build up the practice before you can reliably slough off any other part-time or full-time work. However, all the careful preparation and planning you put into the initial start-up period will be well worth it.

The more you can prepare and plan for your new practice, the quicker you will reap the benefits of all the hard work you've put in. You have most probably heard that 'we never plan to fail, but we frequently fail to plan', and this is never more true than when you've decided to set up on your own.

*To help you on your way*

This book is structured to help your decision-making and planning process as much as possible. You will find brief exercises, decision 'trees' and cost calculators included at various stages. By the time you have worked through this book, you will have had the opportunity to consider the major factors needed to build a successful practice, and will have at your fingertips a complete overview of the costs involved. This will help you to compile your business plan so that you can make any necessary arrangements for a loan. It will also give you a clear idea of how your practice can develop during that all-important first year. And if you have already started your own practice then these sections will help you to plan for growth.

There is also a section at the end of this book which gives full details of various organisations, books, telephone helplines and websites, which are useful sources for further or additional information. These are listed in an easy to use directory format, and include those sources or details which are listed in the text. This is a handy reference section for whatever stage of the process you are currently at.

*Patricia Bishop*

## Acknowledgements

I would like to thank everyone who has helped to shape my thinking and ultimately brought this book into being – my friends, senseis, tutors, mentors, students and family. To Janet Lill for always being there for me. Steven Harold, for being such a supportive colleague and friend. Nicola Martin of the Institute of Clinical Hypnosis for setting me off on this path. My parents Irene and Harry for their unswerving faith in me and support. And lastly my special thanks to my three wonderful sons – Mark, without whose computer skills I would still be struggling now, and James and Chris for making me laugh.

# CHAPTER ONE

# Locating Your Premises

One of the first questions you will need to answer when setting up your own practice is, where?

> **Where should I work from? Does it matter where I locate my practice? Can I work from home? Are there any regulations which affect where I can locate?**

A number of factors need to be taken into account when you are first setting up, as these can directly affect your ongoing costs and how quickly you can build your client base. This section will guide you through the major decisions you need to make and will help you to cost the various options.

**Wherever you choose to locate you will need to consider the following:**

- how much space you need
- whether anyone will be working with you
- your working environment
- how much money you have to spend on rent
- public transport links and car parking facilities
- your personal security and that of your clients
- any legal restrictions which affect your therapy practice
- access for clients with disabilities
- whether to buy, rent, share or use a room in your own house
- whether to work with clients in their own homes
- whether to run a completely mobile practice.

## Size of premises

Do you know how much space you require for your practice? If not, this is one of the first things you need to work out, as this will influence your search for premises and it will save you time and money if you know in advance the minimum amount of space that you need for your work.

> **Knowing the minimum space you require will save you time and money in your search for premises.**

A simple pen and paper exercise is all that is needed to work out the space you need. First, you will need to decide on the minimum amount of equipment that you require in order to be able to work effectively. Next, make a note of how much floor space each piece of equipment requires, for example, the floor space for the chairs you will use. Then, using squared or graph paper, cut out a template for each piece of equipment using an appropriate ratio or scale, eg one square $= 10$ cm$^2$. Arrange these templates into a layout which you might use for your work, for example, a massage couch in the centre of the layout with a few chairs at the side. Make sure that you have allowed adequate space to move around the equipment with ease – one metre is a good standard to allow. Then try a few different layouts. When you have settled on what works best for you, calculate the total space you require (in square metres). If you lay the templates out on a sheet of squared or graph paper, it should be a simple matter to work out the minimum space required, and you can then work out what the best, or optimum, size and layout would be for your practice.

To make this task even easier you might like to check out some of the bigger DIY companies such as B&Q and Sainsbury's Homebase. Both these companies produce catalogues for kitchen layouts which include a design grid. Even more helpful are those office furniture suppliers such as IKEA which supply business equipment catalogues that include both a design grid and also sticky labels sized to represent various pieces of office equipment (for contact details see Chapter 12).

**Make a note of your space requirements here:**

**Minimum size =**                                          **Optimum size =**

Ideally, the room should be large enough to suit both your initial needs *and* whatever growth you can reasonably expect over the course of your first year. Therefore you may want to include provision for a small waiting room and extra chairs, or allow extra space for using the room for training purposes.

### *Reception areas and waiting rooms*

You may be fortunate enough to operate from premises with a general reception or waiting area which you can use. If not, and you can't afford the space for a separate waiting room, then you will need to make some provision for managing clients who arrive either early or late for appointments. And what about those clients who want to bring friends or family along to wait with them?

To get around this problem you could try investigating whether there is some general space within the premises where you could place a couple of chairs, where your clients can be away from the general flow of people through the offices, but close enough to where you are working to be manageable. Another alternative is to allow extra time at the end of each client session (in my experience 30 minutes is best). If your clients are punctual then you will have some welcome free time in which to catch up on your phone calls, take a short break, or have a quick snack – and if they are late, you have already made some allowance for this so the situation becomes less stressful for all concerned.

## Licences

Some therapies may need to be licensed by the local authority.

Depending on the nature of your work and where you are located, you may need to apply to your local authority for a licence in order to set up your practice. For example, the premises that massage therapists work from need to comply with certain legal requirements, such as the need for washable walls and floors so that any oil spillages can be effectively dealt with. Also, in London, massage therapists need to comply with the London Local Authority Act 1991 – Special Treatment Premises.

For further information about the need for your premises to comply with Health and Safety legislation, or for details of who to contact for further information regarding licences or permissions to practise, see Chapter 4.

## Access for disabled clients

The Goods and Services Provision, Part III of the Disability Discrimination Act (DDA) 1995, comes into force on 1 October 2004. This will affect any service provider where 'physical features make access to their services impossible or unreasonably difficult for disabled people'. (source: DDA Code of Guidance)

Wherever you choose to locate, it is important that you review how accessible your premises are for anyone with a disability. Can a wheelchair user, or someone with restricted mobility, access your services? From 1 October 2004, *access* will include access to toilets, car parking and information, and not just the ability to access your practice rooms. A service provider cannot claim exemption from these provisions of the Act on the basis of the small size of their practice or business – it will affect everyone regardless of size.

There are no exemptions for service providers on the basis of their size.

The DDA currently requires service providers to make 'reasonable adjustments' for disabled people, such as providing extra help or making changes to the way they provide their services. If you are already occupying rooms with limited access, or this is all you can find or afford for your first year in practice, you will need to take some commonsense steps to overcome any access difficulties. You could consider the following:

◆ locate your practice on the ground floor
◆ provide a wheelchair ramp if necessary
◆ be prepared to assist a client with disabilities
◆ consider offering a home visit if this is suitable.

Whatever steps you take to make your service more accessible to people with disabilities, you must keep in mind that you are not allowed to offset the costs of any changes by charging a disabled client more for your services than you would anyone else.

If you are still in less than accessible premises after 1 October 2004, you will have to consider making 'reasonable adjustments' to the 'physical' features of the premises in order to overcome any physical barriers to access. Obviously, if you are operating out of your own premises, you will be responsible for any adjustments. If you are renting premises which have little or no suitable access, then write to your landlord and ask what provision they are making for access for people with disabilities. But don't be complacent, start to look around for other more suitable premises. If your rooms are part of an office block, then it is best to co-ordinate this action with other interested tenants/licensees, as a joint effort will generally gain more attention from your landlord.

> **A lack of funds for making the necessary changes and adaptations will not be an adequate excuse for the lack of suitable access provision.**

Reconciling all of this is currently a difficult issue in the complementary therapy world. Many people are operating out of their own homes, or rented offices, most of which have little provision for access for clients whose mobility is impaired. As with most Acts, the provisions of this particular piece of legislation need testing before it becomes clear how these provisions will be interpreted and applied. However, I don't think any one of us wants to be the first test case.

If you would like further information about the provisions of this Act, see Chapter 12.

## The practice environment

Wherever you choose to work from, *you can help to make your practice a success by carefully considering the environment within which you work.*

Check the following:

♦ the noise levels in your work area
♦ the heating and lighting
♦ how your rooms are decorated
♦ the general comfort level for both you and your clients.

### Noise levels

Check out the external noise that you will be subjected to as you work. If you are working from home you may need to block out sound from noisy teenagers, and if you working within a practice, the noise of other people working, talking in the corridors or having loud mobile phone conversations outside your door. Unless you can come to some other arrangement, you may need to invest in some degree of soundproofing. *This can be quite simple.* Draughtproofing doors, placing a thick rug in the room and using material wallhangings can all help to reduce noise considerably. Noise can also be reduced by taking account of where the room is situated, for example, if you are located on a major road, then it might be best for your practice room to be at the back of the building away from the traffic noise and police sirens. You could also try playing some music quietly in the background to take the edge off any other sounds.

And while you are checking out the noise levels, check to make sure that you and your clients cannot be heard outside of your practice rooms. Most therapy work involves a high degree of confidentiality, so make sure that your clients' conversations and personal information cannot be overheard.

### Heating and lighting

Wherever you set up, make sure that you have some individual control of the heating. If your clients are sitting or lying still for any length of time they can start to feel cold even if the room is heated to the usual 21°C. This is especially important for anyone involved in body work where clients are required to remove some of their clothing. If you can't set the heating for the levels you require you may need to invest in a thermostatically controlled electric heater.

What is the lighting like in your rooms? Do you need to have the room well lit for your work, or would it benefit from more subdued lighting? Again, if the lighting doesn't suit your purposes you may need to invest in some table lamps or uplighters which will shed a softer and more comforting level of light, or some spotlights for key work areas.

### Decorations

Check out the standard of decoration in the rooms. Is all bright and clean, and are any floorcoverings fit for your purposes? If not, this may involve you in extra expense. What colours are the rooms decorated in – are they fairly neutral and light, or dark and womb-like? Which would you prefer if you were the client? And how much will it cost to make any necessary changes?

### *Personal comfort*

Wherever you choose to set up, the basic criteria must be that of comfort for both yourself and your clients. Would you feel comfortable as a client being asked to undergo counselling, or a head massage, or whatever else it is that you do, in your practice room? If not, why not? And once you know why not – make those changes. *If you don't feel comfortable with your work area then some of your frustrations may become apparent to your clients.* In any case you will waste energy by endlessly thinking about how things could be, or maybe by working in a very inefficient manner because you don't have the appropriate equipment for your work.

> **Investing in a comfortable work environment will help your practice to grow, and will help you to save your energy for your therapy work.**

## Security and safety

Wherever you decide to locate the chances are that you will, at some time, need to work outside the usual 9–5 hours, even if this isn't a regular feature of your work. Therefore it is important to check how secure you feel in the premises you will be working from. If these are shared offices in one large building, how will you ensure that your clients have access to the premises whilst maintaining a secure environment? Do you have an intercom security system, or security guards, or a staffed reception area that operates 'out of hours'. If not, you may need to adjust your working hours.

     *Before you decide on your premises, do a bit of fact finding.* Find out whether your premises comply with local fire regulations, and explore the existing fire exits – are any kept locked, are they all fully accessible or do you need to remove rubbish or equipment to get out? Do you know who to contact in the case of an emergency? Does the landlord have an out of hours number for the caretaker, or will you be expected to cope with any crisis on your own? What if one of your clients is taken ill and you have to call for an ambulance? Does the switchboard operate out of hours, or will you need to carry a mobile phone? And how confident do you feel about coping with any of these problems on your own in an otherwise deserted office?

     Also, take a look around the local area. How secure would you feel walking to the train or bus links, or making your solitary way across the car park? What will it feel like doing the same journey on a dark winter night? These are all factors which can have an important effect on your overall security and that of your clients, and will ultimately affect your business for good or bad. Taking some time to review this issue now will save you time and money in the long run, and substantially reduce the potential problems and emergencies you might otherwise face.

## Transport links and parking facilities

Where you choose to locate is very important as this can effectively make or break your practice – the better the access, the more clients you will be able to attract. If at all possible, locate as close as you can to existing rail, tube or bus links, and investigate what provision there is for parking outside or adjacent to your rooms.

> **Locate close to transport links and parking facilities to maximise your client turnover.**

Where you locate will also have an influence on the hours you are likely to work. If you choose to locate near a heavily used commuter link such as a tube or rail station, you are in the best position to take on clients who can make either early morning or evening sessions. More and more people are working flexi-hours, and such a location will allow you to catch the commuter flow. And, if you can manage to locate yourself in a major shopping area, whether the local high street or close to a major supermarket, you are more likely to pick up lunchtime and weekend trade from workers in the local shops as well as the shoppers themselves. In such a location, a well-placed advertising board outside your premises could significantly boost your marketing and the take up of your services.

Clients do pick therapists according to many personal criteria, and a therapist who can fit in with their working hours and who is located close to transport links, or a shopping centre, is likely to score quite high on the criteria list – even though this may seem to you a highly subjective way of choosing a therapist.

## Working on your own or with a colleague

Another point to consider when you are first starting up is whether you will be working on your own or with a friend or colleague. It is best to decide on this issue as soon as possible as this may affect the size of the premises you require, especially if the intention is that both of you will be working in the practice at the same time. Also, you will both need to agree, or at the very least compromise, on where you choose to locate and what the implications of this decision are for your own personal time and working arrangements.

Many therapists choose to work on their own as sole traders because of the freedom this allows, and because it is usually the cheapest and quickest way to set up a business. *Working on your own gives you total freedom in how you run your practice, and you get to choose the direction in which the practice grows and develops.* And, of course, once all the bills are paid anything left over is yours.

Working on your own can, however, be quite a solitary existence. There is no one else to help you out in an emergency and no one to whom you can immediately turn for support and advice. It is, therefore, important that you put together a good network of friends, colleagues, tutors, mentors and general advice contacts for help and support before you set up in practice. These are the people who will help, guide and encourage you through those difficult first years and they will quickly form an important feature of your working life.

### *The pros and cons*

**There can, however, be some benefits from joining together with a like-minded colleague or friend:**

- you can share the ongoing costs of the practice
- you may be able to afford better located or bigger rooms
- more than one therapist in a practice will give the practice a more 'established' feel
- you might be able to offer more than one therapy
- you have a second pair of hands to handle telephone calls and take bookings
- you may be able to cover for each other's holidays.

Despite these benefits, you do need to do some initial soul-searching. If you are both friends as well as work colleagues how will you maintain those boundaries? Sharing with another therapist friend can be helpful, but do ensure that both of you treat this arrangement as a formal business contract. Make sure you have discussed and settled the many issues that such an arrangement can raise before you set up together. In this respect you may find it helpful to formalise the arrangement by having a short legal contract drawn up by a solicitor.

## Travel costs and personal time constraints

When you are setting up for the first time every penny counts, so you will need to budget in terms of both time and money if you choose to locate a significant distance from home.

Locating your practice within your local area can save you both time and money. If you can walk to work you will have no reason for being late, and will not suffer the frustrations of late-running public transport or traffic jams.

As in every business, time is money. So if you decide to do home visits or work from different premises at different times during the week, you will need to take your travel time and costs into account. You will also need to consider the equipment which is essential to your business, whether this is portable, and if so, how much you can personally carry and how much may need to be carried by car. If you can't personally carry everything you need, make sure that you have parking facilities close to the premises.

Also, don't underestimate how tiring travelling to different venues can be. Your travel time forms part of your total working hours, so arrange visits or travel as efficiently as possible. Otherwise you will clock up a lot of unpaid overtime, which is 'empty' time for your business and which could perhaps have been better spent working directly with clients or marketing.

## Working from home

Working from home is the lowest cost option for anyone setting up their own practice.

Working from home is often the first option for many therapists, and it has many advantages:

- you won't incur any travel costs
- you won't waste any time travelling
- you won't have any extra rent to pay
- you may be able to use some of your home equipment eg telephone and computer
- if clients cancel or don't turn up, you'll be able to get on with other things
- you are in complete control of the practice environment.

While this all sounds rather good there are a number of issues you should consider first. Do you have the appropriate space to spare? And is this space which you can have full access to whenever you want, or will the room will be used for other purposes? If you don't have the space to dedicate a room to being your practice room, you may need to consider purchasing some portable equipment, for example, folding chairs and a lightweight folding couch, in order to save space and easily store your equipment away when the room is used for other purposes.

What about your family's needs? Unless you are the sole occupant of your home, have you considered your family's needs or those of your flatmates or sharers? If you have a young family you may need to work around their needs and bedtimes, and this will impose certain limits on your working day. Can you afford to lose the flexibility of being able to offer evening or weekend slots, especially during those first crucial months when you are 'growing' the practice?

Will you feel comfortable having strangers enter your home, and know where you live? And will you be able to ensure that there will be no interruptions while you are working, and that your therapy room will always appear clean, uncluttered and welcoming?

If the answer to these questions is a resounding *yes*, and you've considered the other general environmental and access factors – then go ahead, start organising your room and be sure to get your marketing underway as soon as possible.

If you do decide to work from home, then you will need to inform your local council for council tax purposes. This is unlikely to involve much, if any, extra cost unless you have set aside a specific room, or rooms, for the sole purpose of your business.

## Occupying a slot at a local practice, clinic or health club

**If you can't work from home then this is the next least expensive option.**

Working as part of a local practice, clinic, or health and fitness club is the way many therapists start out. Working this way requires minimal outlay – just the costs of your business stationery plus any supplies which are particular to your therapy practice, for example essential oils, herbal remedies etc. The big ongoing costs such as rent, heat and light and the telephone bills will all be paid by the practice. You will also be able to take advantage of any equipment which is provided with the rooms, such as reclining chairs and massage couches. You may also benefit from a central reception area for your clients to wait in, and a receptionist to book in your clients.

All this allows you to commit to working at your new therapy in a clearly structured and well-defined way, which can be very helpful when you are first setting out and may be juggling the demands of other ongoing work with that of your therapy work. Working alongside other therapists will also provide you with some useful support, and this fact alone may be a very important determinant in where you locate. Therapy work can be a very isolated existence, which can be a bit of a shock to anyone who was previously used to working in a large open plan office. *Having other therapists at the practice will allow you some personal interaction and may help to smooth the transition.*

There are, however, some drawbacks to this way of working. Many practices charge therapists an hourly rate for the rooms whether or not any clients have booked in. Other practices demand a percentage of your takings, and this can be as much as 50%. Some practices operate collectively, and may request that you take a turn on various rotas such as staffing the reception desk and taking client bookings for all the therapists at the centre. There can also be problems regarding the facilities on offer and the standard working practices, for example:

- ◆ the equipment
- ◆ standard length sessions
- ◆ practice politics.

You will need to check whether the equipment supplied with the practice suits your needs. If the couches aren't the right height for you, can they be adjusted? Also, does the practice provide any supplies or do you need to bring your own? If you don't already work to standard session times, will the practice allow you to work in a different way? How will you feel if, in order to maximise your time, you need to work with four clients, each one straight after the other without a break? Do your sessions ever over-run?

Finally, be aware that there may be conflicts with other therapists at the centre engaged in the same work – at worst, involving client 'poaching'; and at best, involving the kind of office politics we've all been subjected to at some point (and which for some of us represented one of the reasons why we left our previous occupations in the first place).

*If you're interested in working this way, then you will need to 'cold' sell yourself to the various practices, health and fitness centres and beauty salons in your chosen area.* You may decide to approach some local to your home, or local to where you currently work, especially if this is in a city or town centre. Personal visits often succeed where a phone call doesn't. Be prepared to give a demonstration of your work; offer a free session; drop off copies of your leaflets, brochures and business cards, and take along copies of your professional certificates, confirmation of your membership of any related organisations and your insurance certificates. It is unlikely that you will be able to negotiate much, if any, of the terms on which you are taken on, so it is essential that you get a chance to assess the feel of the place and decide on what it will be like to work there.

## Working as a complementary therapy practitioner in the corporate sector

This has similar benefits to working within an existing practice as your costs can be kept to a minimum. However the working arrangements, including the variety and quality of the equipment which is provided, can vary quite a lot from one company to the next. So you will need to check this out before you commit to working any sessions at the company. The equipment and the standard of your working environment are likely to be of better quality and more carefully thought out if the company you are going to work in already has a long-term commitment to providing this additional 'perk' for staff.

It is potentially easier to get work within such companies if you are offering a therapy which is particularly geared to dealing with work-related problems, such as stress relief, public speaking, confidence boosting and any technique or process which helps with relaxation and performance enhancement. Make sure any leaflets you produce focus on these key areas and the benefits your therapy can bring to the workforce.

One of the more obvious benefits of working within the corporate sector is the ease with which you can expand your practice. Once the quality of your work becomes apparent you are likely to be sought out, and business people more than most are avid networkers, hence your reputation will spread.

You may need to increase your insurance cover depending on the level of cover requested by the company. Currently the most I've been asked to provide cover for is £5 million, and this has only been requested when I've been doing group work or workshops. It is generally an easy matter to increase your cover with your insurance company and the premiums are not high – so don't let this be a deterrent.

**Some problems can arise with these working arrangements, for example:**

◆ some clients may not want to be seen having a session in the workplace
◆ there could be worries about confidentiality
◆ problems over who pays
◆ the company may set the rate for your work
◆ the working hours are likely to be inflexible
◆ sessions may get interrupted
◆ clients may find it harder to relax during a session in their workplace.

### Overcoming concerns about confidentiality

Because you are working as a therapist within a company, some clients may not trust that any issues or problems that they discuss with you will be treated confidentially. This can be a particular problem for those people who most require your services, the workers who are under pressure from management and/or those who have constant tight deadlines to meet. Such workers will often worry that having a session with you will be admitting to the fact that they can't cope with their jobs and need help. To get around this problem try addressing the issue direct by mentioning this particular problem in your leaflets or brochures. If the workforce realise you are aware this could be a potential issue, then they are much more likely to accept that you will treat their issues in a confidential and supportive way. You may also want to make provision for working with some clients in a practice area removed from the workplace, as this may be a better arrangement for them.

If the company sets the rate for your work make sure that you are getting adequate recompense for the time you spend both working at, and travelling to, the site. Even if you are not earning as much as you would like from this arrangement, you may decide that any shortfall is offset by the marketing potential of being located in a large company. However, it is unlikely that you will be able to offer any discounts to certain employees. In some companies, the company may pay a percentage of the session charge, with your client paying the rest. Whilst taken at face value this seems a very generous gesture, it can be counterproductive, as it can bring into question the confidential nature of your work and whether the company will allow you to work on issues other than work related issues if they are paying part of the costs. If there are other therapists working in the company you might want to check with them whether such a policy has affected their work in any way.

Some clients may find it very hard to relax whilst having a session at work, as work issues may be uppermost in their minds. Also it has not been unheard of for employees to be called out of sessions on urgent business. This, plus the likely inflexibility of the hours you may be allowed to work may cause you to consider having another practice area that you can work from, whether this is your own home or whether you choose to investigate working with your clients in their own homes to keep the costs down. In fact, most therapists working within companies have another practice elsewhere.

## Renting rooms

This is a good option for the therapist who has decided to go it alone or in partnership with another therapist. Offices to let are now a common feature, and many are located in central shopping areas served by good public transport links. Most modern day small office lets are by licence, which is a cheap way of settling the contract issues as it rarely involves legal costs of much more than £100; the licences are generally short (one year) and easily renewable, and often you need give just one month's notice in order to quit, thereby minimising your financial commitment. *When you occupy by licence, the business rates are often included in the rent, so the only other cost to you is that of heating and lighting your rooms.*

Shared offices to let will also have shared facilities such as kitchens and toilets. The cleaning and servicing of the common parts, such as entrance areas and corridors, will generally be included in the rent, again reducing your costs. Shared offices can also provide you with a ready pool of people wanting your particular services.

Check that you will have 24-hour, seven-day a week access, so that you can run your practice as flexibly as possible. Also, check that your particular therapy will be allowed, for example, your landlord may have a personal dislike of hypnotherapy. You will need to take on full responsibility for the offices, so expect to be held responsible for locking up and setting burglar alarms as necessary.

## Buying a practice

**Buying a practice is the most expensive option for someone newly setting up.**

Buying a practice is the most expensive approach for someone who is just setting out, as it demands a huge financial outlay. Unless you are taking over an existing practice with a good reputation and are planning to run it along similar lines, be careful. You will need to be very sure of your own skills and abilities. This can be a very risky financial venture even if you've had previous experience of running an office. If there are a number of you joining together to set up the practice, do a 'trial run' of your working arrangements first to see how realistic your venture is. Whichever lender you approach for a loan is going to want to examine your business plan in detail, so you need to be sure that you can carry this off.

*If you want to invest your money in your business, it might be a better option to do so by moving house to something bigger and better located, and which you can work from.*

## How to find your practice rooms

Unless you've decided to work from home, or have some good contacts who can set you up in practice, you will need to search for those premises best suited to your needs. If you've decided to rent or buy, there are a number of ways in which you can further your search in the location you've decided upon:

◆ scan the ads in the local newspapers and local 'free' newspapers
◆ contact local estate agents who deal with both residential and commercial sales/lets
◆ walk around the area, taking a note of shops or offices for sale or to let
◆ put out a request for premises, or information, to any therapy egroups you belong to

- check complementary therapy websites for any offers
- scan the ads in therapy journals.

If you've decided to try for a slot in an existing practice, or to hire rooms for a set time slot, the process is similar, however the more personal your approach the more chance of success you will have. Try the following:

- ring round the practices in your area
- contact beauty salons, hairdressers and fitness centres
- put your request to any therapy egroups you belong to
- contact complementary therapy websites and place an ad
- scan the ads in therapy journals.

Some beauty salons and fitness centres may already have therapists on-site. Enquire whether all the available slots have been taken. Also, check to see whether there is anyone offering your particular therapy – if not, use this fact to help you in your negotiations for space.

This is one of those occasions when your personal network may well deliver the goods for you – so flex those interpersonal muscles. Talk to as many people as you can, and let them know that you are searching for premises. You may be surprised where some of the leads take you, but keep an open mind and check out all the possibilities. Make sure you keep a record of the contacts you have made in order to avoid ringing the same person twice. Sometimes the contacts will tell you that a room or space will be available at a later date – make sure you take details of this and make a note in your diary to ring back nearer the time.

> **Be persistent, plan your search and allocate a certain amount of time to spend on this each week and you should soon have those rooms you've been looking for!**

## Working with people in their own homes

Rather than choosing to work from a specific area or location, you may choose instead to offer your services to people in their own homes – a truly mobile service. A number of therapists offer their services in this way, which of course cuts out completely any premises costs. However, it is generally only successful if you own a car and you ensure your equipment can be easily transported – no one is happy to keep carrying massage couches up to flats on the second or third floor or above.

The following is a breakdown of both the advantages and disadvantages of this way of working.

### The advantages

- no premises costs
- no utility bills
- the working arrangements can be completely flexible
- start-up costs can be kept to a minimum
- your clients might be more relaxed in their own home
- most clients would regard this as an 'added value' service.

### The disadvantages

- you may spend a lot of time travelling, setting up and dismantling equipment
- all your equipment will need to be portable
- personal wear and tear
- other people, children and pets could prove to be a distraction for yourself or client
- you will need to give more thought to your own personal safety
- you may find the setting to be unsuitable for your purposes or therapy
- you will need to be very flexible about your working hours
- your client may not be in when you arrive for the session.

## How will working with people in their own homes work for me?

### How affordable is it?

This is the next cheapest option for setting up your own practice if you choose not to work from home. However, what you save on premises costs and utility bills may well be spent on travel costs, chiefly your petrol, car insurance, road tax and maintenance costs, so make sure you reflect this in your charges. You will need to insure your car for business purposes and this will generally cost more than your usual domestic-use insurance. Also, you will need to set a sum aside for repairs, as the increased use of your vehicle is going to mean more maintenance. If you are often on the road you may also find you will need to pay more for your communication costs because of the increase in your mobile phone calls. However, you can keep this to a minimum if you use your landline and laptop for accessing your emails rather than your mobile. You should also check out what inclusive deals your service provider may offer to businesses 'on the move'.

### How flexible is this way of working?

Whether you live in a rural area or a town or city environment, there will always be people who would prefer to have any services come to them, rather than the other way around. And although this way of working can be highly flexible, you will have to be more open to your clients' availability as they will be asking you to work with them at their convenience and therefore you may not always be able to combine working with two or three clients in a particular area on the same day. You will also need to set your own limits regarding how far you are prepared to travel to see clients.

### What equipment will I need?

The only differences in terms of equipment between setting up a static practice and working with people in their own homes is that whatever you purchase needs to be as easy to carry as possible. This may mean that you have to spend more on some pieces of equipment, for example, to get a light but sturdy folding massage couch; but the good news is that if you decide later on to set up from your own home, or to rent a room, you will not have to duplicate these items. It also means that you can still work flexibly by offering clients sessions in their own home while you build your static practice.

### How can I ensure my safety?

This is perhaps the biggest potential problem associated with this method of working. Although you may have spoken to your client on the phone and decided they sound very pleasant and affable, when you turn up for the session you don't know who else may be there. It is very important that you go with your instincts regarding your client from the time of that very first contact, if something feels wrong have a 'get out' speech prepared. Far better that you lose money than risk your own safety. That said, having talked to therapists I know who work this way there have hardly ever been any incidents of note.

**Go with your instincts – if you feel something is wrong don't feel obliged to hold that session.**

**To safeguard yourself further, the following are some commonsense measures you may like to adopt.**

♦ If you are female therapist, you may decide to only offer your services to other women.

♦ Before going out to work, make sure that you have left a duplicate list of all your appointments for the day, complete with addresses and contact details, in a safe place where a friend or family member would know to find them.

♦ Find out from the client in advance whether there will be anyone else in the home while you are working with them.

♦ Leave your mobile switched on when you enter the client's home with an appropriate number up on the display ready to dial should there be any problems. And keep your mobile switched on until you have gone through the initial note-taking part of your session and have had a chance to more closely review the client's problems, their state of mind and your general safety within this environment.

♦ Take some classes in self-defence.

### Added value

Don't forget that by providing your services in this way you are adding value for both yourself and your client. Taking your services to a client is providing the client with that little extra something: a tangible benefit by virtue of the fact that your client doesn't have to travel, thereby saving them time, money and inconvenience – and the intangible benefit of being 'valued', with all the good subconscious messages that can send out, by the very act of this service coming to them.

This could also prove to be a good marketing point for your practice, especially if no one else in your area is offering a mobile service for your particular therapy. Not only will you be complying with the accessibility requirements of the Disability Discrimination Act, but if you provide your vehicle with some removable signboards or have some professionally made signs on display in your vehicle advertising your services, your daily work schedule can become an effective advertising round.

## The truly mobile office

This is an idea which has achieved greater success in the US than the UK generally due to the size of the vehicles involved, but it is still a concept worth considering. To set yourself up as a truly mobile service you first need to acquire a suitable vehicle. Some people have converted old ambulances, others have gone for even larger vehicles. But whichever vehicle you decide on it will need to already have the following attributes, or be able to be readily converted:

◆ sufficient headroom for yourself and any clients to walk around unhindered in the vehicle
◆ be soundproofed and insulated
◆ have adequate heating and ventilation
◆ be large enough to hold all your equipment with ease and allow adequate space to work
◆ have wash facilities if appropriate
◆ have steps or a hydraulic ramp so that clients can easily enter the therapy area.

It may sound a strange concept, and perhaps appear less manageable given the average size of UK roads compared to those in the States – but it does have some clear advantages:

◆ you are totally in control of your working space
◆ once equipped you only have your ongoing maintenance, fuel and phone bills to pay
◆ you can take your therapy to the client
◆ such a mobile service can be a unique selling point
◆ the sides of the vehicle can be used as mobile advert boards
◆ you can, with permission, park up at sports centres, golf clubs and supermarkets and offer your services direct.

The only disadvantages would seem to be:

◆ being able to afford and equip a suitable vehicle
◆ finding a space to park it outside your home or where you want to work
◆ having to pass another driving test if your current licence doesn't cover the vehicle
◆ possible reluctance from members of the public to try this new concept.

If you decide to explore this option, you will, of course, also need to invest in a full range of mobile communication devices so that you can deal with your phone calls, faxes and emails as you move from place to place.

# CHAPTER TWO

# Equipping the Practice

## Equipping your practice as cheaply as possible

**You may be surprised once you've worked through this chapter at just how little equipment you really need in order to get your practice up and running!**

### *Where are you working from?*

If you are sharing a practice or hiring a time slot at an existing practice or clinic, most of the equipment you require should be available through the room hire. This will keep your initial equipment costs low as the only extras will be your phone, business stationery and general office supplies. However, if you're working from your own home, rented rooms, or even in a mobile capacity, whilst your initial equipment set up costs will be greater with a bit of careful planning these can be kept to a minimum.

### *Equipment – five golden rules*

Whichever way you decide to work, any equipment which you purchase should be evaluated for:

◆ efficiency
◆ ease of transportation
◆ multi-purpose use
◆ durability
◆ its importance to your work.

### *How efficiently can your equipment be used?*

Even if you usually work from home, there will still be occasions when you need to work at other locations, for example, attending meetings or for training purposes. Therefore it is always a good idea to *ensure that whatever equipment you buy can be used flexibly.* This might mean that if you keep all your client records or training notes on computer that you invest in a laptop computer rather than a stand alone version, so that no matter where you are working you can always have your notes with you. Similarly, to keep costs down and to ensure you can work flexibly you might decide it's more efficient to use your mobile phone as the main number for your business, or to buy a folding massage couch so that you can restore a room in your house back to its original purpose at the end of the working day.

Keep flexibility in mind if you are sharing a room with a colleague, or hiring your room out during the time you are not using it. For what suits you may not suit others. Therefore make sure that all your equipment is as adjustable as possible. This may mean that you spend more initially on some equipment such as a massage couch, in order to get one which you can adjust to different heights. However, you may be able to save on other equipment by being able to double up on the uses you can put it to, for example, using a small table which has extendable legs as a coffee table when you are working with your clients, and then extending it to become a desk for writing up notes.

Make sure your equipment is as versatile as possible both for ease of use and for quick transformations of rooms. A room divider on castors can be easily pushed against a wall to open out the room and increase the working space, folding chairs for extra visitors can be brought out when needed. This can be of particular importance if you practise more than one therapy, or share rooms, and frequently have to rearrange the room to suit your needs.

*Make your equipment work for you as much as possible.* If you teach yoga or relaxation you could consider buying chairs where the chair pads are in one piece and removable and therefore can become floor mats for your students to lie down on. If you are sharing your room with another therapist you will both need space to keep your documents or products safe and secure, and therefore you might choose to buy two small lockable filing cabinets which could stack one on top of the other, rather than one large one.

### How flexibly can your equipment be used?

Don't forget that if you use equipment which can fold away when not in use, you can use the walls of your room for extra storage. This can save you considerable space and could allow you to work from a smaller and possibly cheaper room. Using the walls means you could have shelves for books instead of a bookcase, a folding table instead of a desk; hooks on the wall for coats and for storing folding chairs, wall lights instead of floor standing uplighters.

You are only really limited by your imagination, so be creative and really think about how you could use every piece of your equipment in the most efficient and flexible way, and then check out the various suppliers to see what is on offer (for more details of suppliers see Chapter 12).

> **Remember, if you can double up the use of some of your equipment, you have effectively halved the cost of that equipment.**

### How easily can your equipment be transported?

Whether you are operating from your own home or offering a truly mobile service visiting clients in their own homes, there will always be times when you need to move equipment around. *Therefore you need to consider how easy it is to carry any large items of equipment that you require for your business.* For example, it's no good buying a sturdy massage couch if it's too heavy or cumbersome for you to lift in and out of your car, carry on public transport or tote up several flights of stairs. The same principles need to be applied to equipment seemingly made for people on the move. I'm sure I'm not the only person who positively wilts at the thought of having to carry my laptop plus a case load of files around with me all day. The solution to this can be to get a trolley suitcase, the sort air steward/ esses take on their flights, and let the wheels take the strain instead of your back.

If you are constantly on the move you may find it worthwhile to invest in suitable adaptors so that you can use your mobile phone hands-free whilst driving. Some suppliers produce equipment specially for people working whilst on the move. Check out what accessories or equipment may be available for making working from your car more comfortable.

### How easily can your equipment be stored?

Whatever you need to transport around with you, you will also need to store somewhere, whether this is at home, in your practice rooms or in the boot of your car. *Where are you going to keep your equipment and does it all fit in?* If you are frequently on the move with your therapy equipment make sure you have adequate space to store all the necessary items in the boot of your car. Although you can keep some of your equipment on the back seat this is not ideal. Your insurance company is unlikely to pay for equipment which was stolen from your car when it was in full public view. If storage in your own home is a problem you might want to consider storing some of your larger and more robust pieces of equipment in your garden shed, or even in your garage – but do make sure that wherever you store your equipment that the storage area is weatherproof and lockable.

### Can your equipment multi-task?

As well as considering how mobile and adjustable your equipment is, also consider whether you can combine several pieces of equipment in one. Why buy three pieces of equipment if one can fulfil all three purposes? A good example of this is multi-purpose computer equipment, such as the printer/scanner/fax/copier machines currently on the market. Not only do you save on the equipment cost, but you also save on the space you require for this equipment in your work area – which is a definite bonus. Similarly, instead of buying individual items of telephone equipment, investigate the cost of getting your phone, fax and answer machine all as one package.

If you already have some items of equipment or are going to be using some of your existing household equipment, check out how this can best work for you. For example, instead of buying an answerphone you may find you can use your phone service provider's additional services such as free answerphone services (both BT and NTL have a free answerphone service). These services can usually be enhanced for a small fee (generally about £1 a month) to include the remote retrieval of your messages when you are away from home and the upgraded service will also allow you to record your own personalised message. Some phone service providers, such as BT, allow you to have a second phone number and handset operating on the same line but which rings in a distinctive way in order to distinguish certain calls from your usual landline number. You may find this particularly helpful if you are running your practice from home, as the charge for this service is cheaper than installing and renting a second line.

If you are thinking about purchasing a fax machine but already have a computer and modem connection, check whether you can send faxes via your modem. Unless you are faxing documents which are not produced on your computer on a regular basis, you may find that the facilities on your computer are adequate for your initial needs.

### How durable and safe is your equipment?

Whatever equipment you buy for your practice needs to be durable and therefore of good quality. *It is a false economy to invest in cheap and possibly substandard equipment.* If you are not sure of the best standards for your particular therapy, ask around amongst your colleagues and tutors. Don't forget that your equipment does not have to be new, so do check out any secondhand suppliers as you may be able to get better equipment for a lower price if you are prepared to work with equipment which is not new.

If you are purchasing secondhand electrical equipment, such as computer equipment, check to see if any guarantees are offered – this is more likely to be the case if you are buying equipment from a secondhand dealer rather than an individual. Also, check which applications are already installed, as this could save you further expense and time – and make sure that the hard disk has been wiped of any previous information.

The internet auction site, eBay, is a good place for checking out secondhand items such as massage couches and basic office equipment. If you order anything through this site the only additional costs will be for delivery or postage and packaging – but do check these out before you buy in order to ensure that you are not paying more for delivery than you've paid for the item.

As all of your equipment is going to have to stand up to some heavy use. You may want to ensure that any chairs you buy have been tested for durability and also for the weights that they can support – this can be of special interest if as part of your therapy you will be working with people to help them lose weight.

> **Remember – your equipment is your responsibility so make sure that it is safe and fit for purpose.**

### Do you really need that item?

It's worth spending some time at the outset to look long and hard at what you actually *need* as opposed to indulging in some business 'retail therapy'. Carefully consider what you already have and how you could creatively use any new pieces of equipment in order that you can double up on the purposes you can put these to. If you have some items in mind which are *desirable* rather than essential, keep these on your business 'wish' list to indulge in once your business has taken off and you can afford these items.

> **Don't be tempted to indulge in business 'retail therapy'.**

## Setting a theme

Unless you are working from rooms in an existing practice or clinic, where the colour schemes and equipment are already decided, you will have the opportunity to choose your own theme. Setting a theme in your practice can be another form of branding and a way in which your particular therapy or products are known. If you choose a co-ordinating or complementary colour scheme for your room and the equipment and furniture used in the room, you are sending out subliminal messages of comfort, uniformity and integrity, which you can use to enhance your professional image. This doesn't mean that all your equipment needs to be brand new or bought from the same range, but it does mean that you give some careful thought to how it is presented and therefore how your clients will respond to it. You can further increase the personal 'branding' effect by following through on your chosen colour scheme so that it even includes the towels you use, or your mugs and pens – and if you have these latter items overprinted with your practice details, these visual cues can help to reinforce your professional status and raise your business profile. *Research has shown that a business identity is important.*

## Business equipment and furniture suppliers

Whilst you may already have various companies in mind for supplying your furniture and equipment, you may find it useful to check out some of the business suppliers as well. You will find these listed in your local directories. Check out the different equipment and furniture catalogues they produce both for the prices and for the variety of goods they have on offer. For example, you will generally find that a business supplier will carry a larger range of telephones, fax machines or computer printers, and you may find this helpful if you are looking for flexible use at minimum cost (for further details of business equipment and furniture suppliers see Chapter 12).

## What equipment, furniture and supplies does your practice need?

**You will need to review your requirements against the following:**

◆ specialist equipment and furniture
◆ general equipment and furniture
◆ computer and telephone equipment
◆ business stationery
◆ office supplies
◆ business environment purchases.

## What specialist equipment will you need?

The specialist equipment you require will vary according to the particular therapy or therapies that you are engaged in. Most 'talking' therapies, such as counselling or psychotherapy, will not require any special equipment, just comfortable armchairs. However, anyone engaged in massage work or healing will also need to invest in a massage couch or treatment table. Other therapies may require items such as exercise mats or sound equipment.

Take a long, hard look at the minimum you require in order to run your practice and then invest in the best you can afford. *You should not be expecting to replace any specialist equipment for at least three years (five years is the optimum) so choose wisely.* How flexible, or adaptable, is the equipment you need? For example, if you are thinking of purchasing a massage couch, can you vary the height of the working surface to suit both your needs and those of anyone you may be sharing this equipment with? If you're travelling to your clients you will need to find out how much the massage couch weighs. Can you carry the couch out to your car easily? How easy is it to fold?

### Don't forget your clients' needs

As well as considering how the equipment suits your needs, don't forget to consider your clients' needs. For example, is your massage couch wide enough for most clients to rest on without their arms flopping over the sides? How will a less able person be able to use your equipment? Will you need to provide a set of steps, or a hand rail? Remember what you have learnt during your training about disability and access issues and put these ideas into action.

When you have decided on the specialist equipment you need, jot it down. **You might find it helpful to keep a running total of your equipment needs and costs in the table on page 30** (Figure 1). Please note the items listed are just a prompt to get you thinking about what you might need, your therapy may require additional equipment so adjust the table to reflect your requirements.

| Specialist equipment | Cost |
|---|---|
| massage couch | |
| couch carrybag | |
| couch covers | |
| pillows and towels | |
| exercise mats | |
| sound system | |
| reclining chair | |
| other items | |
| Total | £ |

Figure 1. Specialist equipment costs.

## What general equipment do you need?

**Generally the minimum amount of equipment for most therapies will be:**

◆ three chairs
◆ a small table
◆ a small, lockable filing cabinet
◆ somewhere for your client to hang their coat.

Three armchairs are the ideal minimum, as this allows one chair for the therapist, one for the client and one for any person (partner, family member or friend) the client may bring with them. If possible, you may also want to invest in an extra chair which is solidly constructed, has a more upright position with a higher seat and without arms. This sort of seat will be more accessible for anyone who finds a low seat difficult to get in or out of, it will also prevent any potentially embarrassing situations if your client is too large to be able to fit into your usual armchairs.

A small table is ideal for holding cups or tissues. You can also use it to rest your notes on, or as a surface for your client to write or draw on. If you are going for an initial minimal approach to your equipment purchasing, a table can be used to break up the starkness of the environment and you can soften the effect by placing a vase of flowers on the table.

It is a requirement under the Data Protection Act 1998 that client records are kept securely. If you are sharing a room with other therapists you will need to make sure that your clients records are held safely and the best way of ensuring this is to get a metal lockable filing cabinet. You can also use the cabinet for storing any of your business stationery, CDs and tapes, or small office supplies which you don't want cluttering the room.

Phone several suppliers to get prices for the equipment you need, in order to make sure you are getting a good deal for your money. **Once you have decided on your requirements, fill in the table below (Figure 2) so that you have a record of your potential expenditure on general equipment and furniture.**

| General equipment and furniture | Cost |
|---|---|
| armchairs | |
| chairs | |
| table/s | |
| desk | |
| bookcase or shelves | |
| filing cabinet | |
| coatstand | |
| clock | |
| kettle | |
| mugs | |
| glasses | |
| spoons | |
| other | |
| | |
| Total | £ |

Figure 2. General equipment and furniture costs.

**As your practice grows so you can always invest in extra pieces of equipment or furniture – but think small and flexibly to begin with so that you get the maximum use out of your investment.**

## Computer equipment

If you don't already have a computer and printer, these could be one of your best investments. Not only will you be able to create and print your own business stationery, if you so choose, but if you add on a modem or have a computer with an integral modem, then for the price of a phone call you can access the internet and send and receive emails.

If you don't know much about computers then get a knowledgeable friend or family member to help you make your choice, or at least help you to decide on the kind of package that will work best for you as you set up your business. Buying computer equipment is expensive, but there are some very good packages on offer which include a computer of a good specification, usually with an integral modem, CD writer and with appropriate business applications preloaded. Such packages usually include a basic printer and scanner and are therefore more than adequate to meet your initial set up needs.

You can, of course, buy secondhand computer equipment, but you will need to *ensure that this is coming from a reputable source*. Make sure you investigate whether there are any guarantees available, so that if the equipment breaks down soon after purchase you are not left with a sizeable bill for repairs.

### Other equipment

As well as your computer hardware you will need to invest in a computer desk and a suitable chair – unless of course you decide to go for a laptop rather than a stand alone computer. Make sure that whatever desk you buy you have sufficient room both for your computer and your papers and notes, as well as space for any printer or scanner (buying a combined model will help to save space). You may also need to get a footrest or a desk lamp in order to make working at the computer a more comfortable experience. There are guidelines for the correct siting of computer equipment and for the correct seating principles to adopt. For further information, see Chapter 11.

Whether you keep all this equipment in your practice room will depend on how and where you work. If there is insufficient room within your practice you will need to allocate some space in your home. You need to consider this carefully as it will mean that you won't be able to complete all your work at your practice – do you want to be bringing some of it home to do? If not, it might be better to invest in a laptop so that you can get most of your work done wherever you are.

If you buy computer equipment you will also need to invest in some shelves or a cupboard for all the paper, business stationery, CDs, floppy discs and print cartridges you are going to need and use.

### Buying a laptop

If you are working with clients in their own homes, or if you regularly work at different locations, it would be advisable to get a laptop rather than a stand alone computer as your main computer. Once you've bought your laptop you can then shop around for a mobile phone which can link to your laptop either by means of bluetooth wireless technology or via a USB cable and port. This will allow you to dial in to download your emails. If you then work off-line compiling your replies and only dial in again to send your responses, you will be keeping your costs to a minimum. Once you get home you can simply plug your laptop into your landline or broadband connection in order to access the internet in the most cost-effective way.

If you've bought a laptop then it could be worth your while to take out insurance on it. You are going to be carrying it around with you so it is much more likely to have to withstand some knocks and harsh treatment. If you are trying to keep your costs within a manageable budget, having insurance to cover the cost of repairs to your laptop could help considerably.

### Buying for the future

Make sure that whatever computer equipment you purchase is going to meet your needs for the next three years at least. *Think hard before you buy about exactly what you are going to use it for.* For example, will it just be for writing up notes and correspondence, researching and downloading files from the internet, or will you be thinking of creating and printing your own business stationery, designing your website or recording your own CDs? If you are thinking of the former as being your main use for this equipment, then you simply need to invest in a good PC with a reasonably fast modem or broadband connection, and a printer. However, if you are thinking in terms of using your equipment for creative or design purposes, then you may want to extend your equipment requirements to include a scanner, digital camera, microphone, good quality colour printer and some appropriate design-based software. If you think you are going to be spending a large amount of your time on the computer everyday, make sure you get a model which can deal with the workload.

Also think about the future and how you may want to use this equipment in a few years' time. For example, if you are a life coach and are thinking about more flexible ways of working, you might want to put a webcam down on your wish-list as a means of speeding up your responses and yet keeping your contact with your client as personal as possible. *Whatever equipment you choose always go for the best specification that you can afford.* Things change fast in the computer world – having a good specification machine should prevent you from frequently having to upgrade your equipment.

### Modem versus broadband connections

If you are going to use the internet a lot, or transfer very large files on a regular basis, you may want to consider having broadband access installed in your home or practice. Although it is more expensive, you will save a lot of your time and therefore will be saving money indirectly. Choose carefully where your broadband connection is going to be sited. Unless you have a designated work area, such as a study, for the connection to be installed in, make sure that the connection is installed in an area where you can work fairly quietly without interruptions, and also where it will not disturb others.

**Once you've decided on your computer requirements, list them in the table on page 35 (Figure 3).**

## Telephone equipment

### Working from home

If you are running your practice from home you may find that your home phone and landline is all that you need, although this will depend on how many others in your household use the house phone on a regular basis, as you don't want any potential clients having problems contacting you. If this is the option you decide on you should be aware that some phone service providers do not allow you to advertise what is essentially a home phone number in trade directories such as *Yellow Pages* – so check this out first.

A cordless phone can work very well if you are working from home and do not have a room set aside as your designated practice room. This means that you can take the phone with you into whichever room you are working from; ensures that you can answer any calls in a professional manner, and also means that when you are working the phone can be left outside your room so that your clients are not disturbed and you don't have to worry about unplugging the phone and potentially losing any calls.

| Computer equipment | Cost |
|---|---|
| stand alone PC | |
| laptop | |
| modem | |
| scanner | |
| printer | |
| printer cartridges | |
| multi-purpose scanner/printer/fax/copier machine | |
| CD writer | |
| microphone | |
| digital camera | |
| webcam | |
| USB cable for mobile phone | |
| computer desk | |
| adjustable swivel chair on castors | |
| adjustable footrest | |
| gel wrist rests | |
| adjustable desk lamp | |
| screen filter | |
| copy/document holder | |
| computer software | |
| laptop bag or trolley case | |
| equipment insurance | |
| other | |
| **Total** | £ |

Figure 3. Computer costs.

### Installing a second line

If the telephone traffic in your household is high, you might find it more beneficial to install a second line. As previously mentioned, some phone service providers allow you to have a second phone number and handset operating on the same line but which rings in a distinctive way in order to distinguish business any calls from your usual landline number. The charge for this service is cheaper than installing and renting a second line.

If you are installing a second line at home, or getting a landline installed in your practice room you may want to investigate making this a freephone number. This works as a positive inducement for callers – if they do no have to pay to make an enquiry about your services, a caller may ring you in preference to another complementary health practice which does not have a freephone number.

### Siting your business connections

If you are thinking of installing a second telephone line for your business, setting up a fax or installing broadband for your internet access, make sure that you locate these connections where they can be used effectively – ideally in a designated work area, or a quiet space where any work will be uninterrupted. If you plan on changing the layout of your rooms in order to make space for your practice, decide on your working space as soon as possible and determine how long you are going to be able to use this space for your work – it will cost you extra each time you need to move these connections, so it's better to get it right first time.

### Using an answerphone

Whatever telephone equipment you have, you need to make sure your business calls are still being answered when you're not able to. If you are working from home, it is better that you deal with any business calls direct rather than have a family member answer the phone. If you don't already have one you should be considering investing in a separate answerphone; a telephone with a built in answerphone, or paying your phone service provider to provide an answerphone service. Some service providers offer a free answerphone service, but normally you will not be able to retrieve your messages when you are away from home or out of the office unless you pay a small fee (generally about £1 a month) for an enhanced version of the service – the enhanced version will also allow you to record your own personalised message for callers.

Most telephones with built in answerphones will allow you to filter incoming calls as you can hear who is calling via the loudspeaker as soon as they begin to leave a message. Again, this can be useful if you are working from home and want to avoid callers at certain times, but don't want to miss any members of your family who may be calling.

### Using call divert and call waiting

Wherever you work, you may find it useful to subscribe to the call divert and call waiting services from your phone service provider. Call divert will automatically divert your calls to another designated number, so you could, for example, divert all your business calls from one location to the phone at your next workplace – or alternatively all your business calls could be diverted to your home number. You decide which numbers and when to divert. This will ensure that any calls come through to you direct. You should be aware that you are likely to be charged for the diverted part of the call, so if you are constantly diverting calls to your mobile phone number this can prove to be rather expensive.

Call waiting is another useful service. Whether you are working from your home phone or business phone this allows you to keep a caller on hold whilst you answer another incoming call. It also allows you to move freely between all the callers. This can be particularly useful if you are dealing with a personal call when another call comes in, as it allows you to check the call and deal with it direct if it is a business enquiry.

### Mobile phones

Even if you don't have a mobile phone for your personal use, you might want to consider getting one for your business use especially if you work away from home, or spend time travelling to different work locations or to and from your clients' homes.

*Your mobile phone can also be your sole business number, and the only one which you advertise.* This can work for you in a number of ways – it gets around any problems you might have with your home phone service provider if you advertise your 'home' landline as your business number; it also saves you having to total up your business calls versus your personal calls each month for accounting purposes (this might seem a minor point but you should be aware that it can take an hour or more to add up all the calls each month, and that's an hour's unpaid overtime), and of course, you can be contacted wherever you go without missing calls or paying for diverted calls.

Some mobile phone companies offer good value business packages which may include preferential call rates, free insurance and/or a free replacement handset each year.

Check out the deals on offer. You will need to prove that you are a bona fide business, so you may need to show details of your business bank account. If you are going to use a mobile phone as your main business number it is rarely worthwhile to use a 'pay as you go' option, especially if you are intending to use your mobile phone to access the internet, as the cost per call is usually much higher than calls made on a monthly contract rate.

**Check which particular benefits your mobile handset has before you purchase. For example:**

◆ How long does the battery last on standby and whilst making calls?
◆ What sort of details can you store on the phone and how many?
◆ Can you use your mobile phone with your laptop?

If you use your phone a lot it will make good sense to purchase a model which can last for as many hours as possible between charges – especially if you are frequently on the move. You don't want to have to charge up your phone more than once in a day. Also, if you need to contact your clients while you are on the move, it may make sense to include their details in the address book on your phone. If you have a good number of clients you will need to choose a phone which has a large capacity for storage. And if mobile communications are a must for you, then make sure your phone can be connected to your laptop whether by using the appropriate wireless technology, or a cable and USB port.

If you are always on the move but either don't have, or don't want to carry, a laptop with you all the time, you can arrange to set up your mobile phone so that you can access your emails. However, unless you are always sent very short emails you could find that your account fills up very quickly. It is still a useful option though – so check out how it could work for you.

Even if you don't take out insurance for other items, it is generally a good idea to take out insurance on a mobile phone. It is a sad fact, but mobile phone theft is on the increase, so if you are trying to keep your costs under control it may make sense to include the cost of insurance rather than risk having to meet the costs for a replacement handset.

*It's a good idea to think about replacing your mobile phone every one to two years.* This will enable you to take advantage of any new technological changes and help you to avoid any problems regarding the replacement of batteries. Remember, you do not have to change your number, although some phone service providers effect a small charge for swapping numbers over. You should also be able to get any details that you have stored on your sim card transferred to the new handset, so there should be no need to re-enter any names and numbers you have stored in the address book. If you are more familiar with, or find it easier to use, a particular make of phone, then go for an upgrade of the same make.

## *Fax machines*

A fax machine is not an essential buy when you starting up your practice. But you will find it helpful to invest in one as your business grows. A fax machine will help you to extend the ways in which people can communicate with you, for example, you wouldn't necessarily want to invest in a textphone, but a fax might mean that any clients who are hearing impaired could get in contact with you by fax if they, or you, were unable to send an email. It can also be useful for dealing with other companies, either for placing orders or confirming arrangements or training course details.

**If you do decide to purchase a fax machine, you might want to consider the following:**

◆ getting a plain paper fax rather than thermal roll
◆ multi-purpose machines.

A plain paper fax machine can also be used as a copier for single sheet copying. Also, unlike thermal roll imaging, a plain paper machine means that the image will keep its sharpness and detail, whereas thermal imaging tends to fade with exposure to light – which can be a problem if you need to keep any records for a length of time for legal purposes. It is generally cheaper to load a machine with plain paper rather than buy thermal rolls, although you may want to check this out before you buy.

If you don't already have a phone for your practice you might want to consider buying a combined fax/telephone/answerphone machine in order to keep your costs down. Check that the machine is able to switch between fax (data) and phone (voice) calls automatically and that you can vary the options according to your specific work needs, for example, you will want to be able to switch the machine over to automatically take fax and phone messages when you are working with a client. Make sure that you can pick up any answerphone messages remotely. Some machines also allow you to pick up fax messages remotely but you are unlikely to find this of much use unless you are a serious user.

List your telephone equipment requirements in **Figure 4 below.**

| Telephone equipment | Cost |
| --- | --- |
| phone – cordless | |
| second line | |
| extension handsets | |
| answerphone | |
| mobile phone | |
| socket doubler | |
| fax machine | |
| USB cable for mobile phone | |
| additional services – eg call waiting | |
| equipment insurance | |
| other | |
| Total | £ |

Figure 4. Telephone equipment costs.

## Business stationery

Although not exactly equipment, I've included this section here as it can form a sizeable cost when you are first setting up and equipping your practice.

### *The basics*

You will need to make sure that you have adequate initial stocks to meet your business needs for at least the first month if you are creating and printing your own stationery, or for the first three months if you are using a printing company to produce your stationery. **Whatever your therapy you will need to keep stocks of the following basics:**

◆ headed paper

◆ compliment slips

◆ business cards

◆ any pre-printed receipts

◆ practice brochures

◆ client record sheets

◆ invoices

◆ envelopes

◆ fax header sheets (if applicable).

### Designing your stationery

This can be quite a time-consuming task, so make sure you allow sufficient time for this to be completed in advance of setting up your practice. A good lead time for most things is three months. **Before you start to design your stationery, you will need to have confirmed the following:**

◆ the address you will be working from, or using for correspondence

◆ your telephone number

◆ your fax number

◆ your mobile phone number

◆ your email address

◆ your website address

◆ your NHS provider number

◆ your membership of any professional organisations and official designation.

Once these have been confirmed, then you can decide on fonts, styles, colours and the general layout. You may find it helpful to ask your colleagues for copies of their business stationery, so that you can get a feel for the kind of design you would prefer and what you think works well. Whether or not you print the stationery yourself, you will need to put together a print ready version in your preferred layout and style. Some print companies will offer to do this for you for a small charge, so do some phoning around first.

*If you keep the same, or similar, design for all your stationery this can become your 'brand' and a way in which others will recognise you.* To personalise this further you could design a simple logo which reflects something about you or your work – some people design a logo around their initials or company name, others will use a simple line drawing to convey an aspect of their work. Check how others in your field have advertised their practices – *Yellow Pages* is a good place to start – a lot more can be conveyed with a simple logo.

### Keeping stocks

If you are getting a print company to do your printing, investigate what offers are available for bulk orders in order to keep your costs down. This may mean that you will need to provide extra storage for this stock, so do keep it to practical levels. If you are printing your own stationery then you can operate a 'just in time' approach and keep the minimum possible. For some practices this will mean enough for one week, others one day, and for those who are very well set up the stationery or documents will only need to be printed off when they are needed.

### Suppliers

Depending on how much stationery you use in your practice, and how varied your requirements are, you may find that a trip maybe once a week or once a month to a local stationery retailers is all that is required. If you have any special requirements such as getting your practice details printed on your business folders or mugs, or if you order large supplies of particular items such as padded envelopes, paper, CDs or even couch rolls, you might find you can get a cheaper deal by purchasing through a business stationery suppliers. Local suppliers are listed in the trade directories. Check for any delivery charges before placing an order. Some companies will deliver free of charge if you place an order that exceeds a minimum price. Office suppliers often put together office stationery starter packs at a reduced price which you may helpful. For details of some possible suppliers see Chapter 12.

### Working out costs

**Once you've decided on your stationery needs, cost these out and enter them in the table on page 43 (Figure 5)**. If you extrapolate your costs for a whole year and enter the annual figure this will help you to work through the next chapter – determining how you are going to finance your practice and whether you need to take out a loan. These figures are likely to be guesswork at this stage, but spend some time making them as reasonable a guess as possible.

| Business stationery | Cost |
|---|---|
| headed paper | |
| compliment slips | |
| business cards | |
| pre-printed receipts | |
| practice brochures | |
| client record sheets | |
| invoices | |
| envelopes | |
| fax header sheets | |
| fax paper or thermal rolls | |
| labels | |
| pens, pencils, sellotape, paperclips etc | |
| notepads | |
| A4 white paper | |
| A4 coloured paper | |
| A4 card | |
| other | |
| Total | £ |

Figure 5. Business stationery costs.

## General office supplies

As well as your equipment and stationery, don't forget you may need to keep basic supplies of tea and coffee, various cleaning products and any other basics such as paper tissues or towels, bottled water, soap etc. This is more likely to be the case if you are renting rooms, rather than working from home or within an existing practice or clinic.

You may find that your needs are adequately met by purchasing through a local supermarket or shop, but if time is short, or you order a lot of supplies on a regular basis or you need to have your purchases delivered, you may find it easier to combine an order for these goods with your stationery or equipment purchasing. Many office suppliers will supply goods for the entire range of your business and practice needs, which may help you save time as well as money. Work out your costs in Figure 6 below.

| Office supplies | Cost |
|---|---|
| toilet rolls | |
| cleaning products | |
| couch rolls | |
| tea and coffee | |
| bottled water | |
| soap | |
| paper towels | |
| tissues | |
| other | |
| Total | |

Figure 6. Office supplies costs.

## Business environment purchases

These are the extras that go towards making a more agreeable working environment for both yourself and your client. Extras such as:

◆ plants
◆ pictures
◆ water fountains
◆ air filters

◆ additional heaters to maintain a comfortable working warmth in winter
◆ fans for keeping everyone cool in summer
◆ specialist or variable lighting to help create a relaxed atmosphere, soften the mood or highlight a working area
◆ and fragrances – whether of the plug in variety or burning scented candles, incense or essential oils in oil burners.

I would include with this any building works – major or minor – which could help to improve the environment. For example, soundproofing a wall, partitioning off an area to use as a waiting room, or installing a ramp for wheelchair users. All such improvements will help to make your working environment a better vehicle for your talents and skills.

**List your business environment requirements in Figure 7 and enter the cost or amount that you are prepared to pay in your annual budget for these items.**

| Business environment items | Cost |
|---|---|
| plants | |
| pictures | |
| water fountains | |
| CD/tape player | |
| air filters | |
| ionisers | |
| fans | |
| additional heaters | |
| spotlights, uplighters, table lamps | |
| dimmer switch | |
| candles | |
| incense, essential oils and burners | |
| environmental building works | |
| other | |
| Total | £ |

Figure 7. Business environment costs.

Everything about your practice should reflect you and the way in which you wish to work. This knowledge will come with time, so be prepared to invest in your environment when the time is right – your investment will pay dividends in terms of client satisfaction and will be reflected in the referrals that you receive.

## Planning for growth

Now you have a clearer idea of what your minimum requirements are – think big.

Even though you may only just be setting up, it is still a good idea to speculate a few years into the future. What equipment would you ultimately like to be working with? This could be some completely new pieces of equipment, perhaps extending the way in which you work. For example, if you are thinking of increasing your revenue by selling copies of your guided meditation CD you might want to invest in equipment which will allow you to burn more than one CD at a time. Other items on your 'wish list' may be purchases that will increase your comfort or that of your clients, such as replacing your bottom end of the range massage couch for one which you can adjust to suit your working height and which may be wider or have an increased amount of foam padding. You could also choose to invest in some equipment which may help your efficiency and effective use of time, for example, buying a laptop so that you can work on your correspondence even when you are away from your main practice. Or you could use part of your list for noting which equipment you would like to update and when, in order to keep abreast of new technological developments or simply to keep your equipment to a good standard.

Whatever items you are thinking of, make sure that you incorporate these into your financial plans in order that they can be realised. Keep your wish-list in a safe place and make sure you review it on a regular basis, adding and deleting items as appropriate and as your business needs change.

You may already have listed your potential future purchases in the previous tables, however, you might now find it helpful to review your equipment lists again and extract those wish-list items so that these details are kept separately. The following table (Figure 8) can be used to record these items.

| Future growth items | Cost |
|---|---|
|  |  |
|  |  |
|  |  |
|  |  |
|  |  |
|  |  |
|  |  |
| Total | £ |

Figure 8. Future growth costs.

## Taking this forward

Once you've had a chance to review all your business equipment needs and have costed your requirements, add these figures up in order to arrive at the total cost – *nb ensure you have entered annual figures for all the items or categories*. Now you are ready to transfer these costs to your projected profit and loss account in order to determine whether you will require any extra funding for your first year. All this is explained in the next chapter.

# CHAPTER THREE

# Financing the Practice

Having worked through the previous two chapters, you should now have a clear idea of where you will be working from and the costs involved in working from that location, the minimum amount of equipment you can effectively work with during your initial set-up phase and first year, and will be thinking about whether you want to be working full-time or part-time in your chosen therapy. Now comes the reality check – costing it all out.

## Planning for financial success

**Time spent planning at this stage will quickly pay for itself.**

You may have planned various aspects of your life before, for example, a long holiday or a new kitchen, or you may be a relative newcomer to planning. However, one thing is certain, *a lack of planning at this stage may result in financial problems which could easily have been avoided*. Do you know how much it is going to cost you to start up your new business? And, do you know how much you will need to be earning from your business in that crucial first year in order that you can meet all your outgoings?

Until you have worked out exactly how much money you will need in your first year of business, you won't know how much you might need to borrow, and if you can't produce a solid plan outlining all the relevant details your bank is unlikely to make you any loans that you might require.

Planning your business can be a lot easier than you think. There are six simple steps you need to carry out.

## The six-step planning process

### Step 1 – How much do you really need for living purposes?

A quick way of working this out is to look back over your last three bank or building society statements (include your last three credit card statements as well, if relevant). Now, calculate how much you pay annually for all your personal and household expenses. This will include rent, mortgage and utility bills as well as personal insurances and clothing. For some items, such as 'entertaining', you may need to provide a 'guesstimate' and decide what your future annual budget will be. **Once you have these figures you can enter them in the following table (Figure 9):**

| Personal living costs | Annual cost |
|---|---|
| rent/mortgage | |
| insurances/endowment policies | |
| water rates/fuel bills | |
| council tax | |
| telephone/internet | |
| television licence/cable or satellite costs | |
| food | |
| clothing | |
| entertaining | |
| holidays | |
| birthday and Christmas presents | |
| repairs and maintenance | |
| travel/car | |
| other (eg NI contributions – see step 6) | |
| Total | £ |

Figure 9. Personal living costs.

### Step 2 – How much do your business premises cost?

If you're not going to be working from home, then now is the time to start investigating the cost of renting premises and/or the cost of sharing rooms. Try to get at least three sets of costs that you can compare, and then take the average of the three as your guideline. To these costs you may need to add business rates, water rates, gas and electricity charges, telephone and internet costs and cleaning. You may be able to get some of these figures from your potential landlord, others you will need to guess at. As a general rule, round the costs up rather than down, as most people underestimate their outgoing costs.

Don't forget to add any insurance costs. *Although your landlord may not make any charges for insurance related to any common parts, you will still need to be insured for any claims made by your clients or visitors.* This public liability insurance will generally be included within your professional indemnity insurance (see step 4 below). If it isn't you will need to arrange for this separately. You will, of course, also require your own office contents insurance, to guard against the risk of loss in respect of any break-ins or damage. **Once you've worked out these figures, enter them in the table below (Figure 10).**

| Business premises costs | Annual cost |
|---|---|
| rent or cost of hiring a practice room | |
| business rates | |
| water rates | |
| gas and electricity charges | |
| telephone costs | |
| internet costs | |
| cleaning | |
| insurance premiums | |
| other | |
| Total | £ |

Figure 10. Business premises costs.

### Step 3 – What are your equipment costs?

If you've worked through the checklist in Chapter 2 you should already have a clear idea of what equipment you will need for your first year. Now it's time to add in the figures if you haven't already done so. Ring round suppliers to get quotes for equipment and/or copies of office, medical and specialist suppliers catalogues, and use these for your equipment costings.

Remember to take a strategic view of all your needs, so you may want to complete two lists: one for the essential equipment you will require to start the business, the second for equipment for which you can wait a bit longer before purchasing, for example, items which might help the business run more smoothly or efficiently such as extra chairs for visitors or the waiting room.

As well as the essential equipment, don't forget to cost your initial business stationery needs such as pens, paper, printer ink, diary, business cards etc. Some office suppliers offer a starter pack which may be helpful, but check that you will be using all the products before you decide to purchase. If you are going to get your letterheads, compliment slips and business cards professionally printed, rather than printing your own, you will need to ring round for some quotes.

Don't forget that the equipment you purchase when you set up will eventually require replacing. If you can afford it at this stage it's a good idea to plan for it by building an aspect of this into your budget now. Add an extra 20% to the figures, as most equipment and furniture should last for between three to five years before it needs replacing. **Use Figure 11 below to work out your costs.**

| Equipment costs | Annual cost |
|---|---|
| general business equipment and furniture | |
| specialist therapy equipment and furniture | |
| computer equipment | |
| telephone equipment | |
| business stationery | |
| general office supplies | |
| business environment purchases | |
| business equipment insurance | |
| wish-list items | |
| other | |
| | |
| Total | £ |

Figure 11. Equipment costs.

### Step 4 – *What are your professional and legal costs?*

You may already be a member of a professional organisation, or have yet to join any. But in any case you do need to make an allowance for these costs. Ask around amongst your colleagues and tutors to find which professional bodies offer the best 'value for money' memberships. Most professional organisations will have a referral list of their practising members which they make available to the public, which could help with your advertising costs. Also, many organisations offer a cheap deal on professional insurance for their members. Others may also be good for the help and support they offer their practitioners and may also produce monthly or quarterly newsletters which can be an additional resource for techniques, or updating skills and additional training. Included in this support may be contact details for email help and advice, or an egroup for discussion and informed debate on related issues.

Depending on the therapy you are practising, *you may be professionally obliged to belong to a particular organisation in order for you to be able to practise*, as that particular organisation may be responsible for setting the standards for your profession. Choose your membership wisely. Although it appears more professional to belong to more than one organisation, for initial purposes limit yourself to joining a maximum of two professional bodies.

As well as membership costs, you will need to be insured for your professional liabilities. You will need to take out professional indemnity insurance (this covers you for any legal action being take against you) and public liability insurance (this covers you for any accidents that a client may have whilst on your premises, eg tripping and falling over and any subsequent damages that may be incurred). The minimum cover you should consider is £2 million, with £5 million being the initial maximum. The most I've ever been asked for is £5 million cover, and this has been when I've been working for government agencies doing training or holding one-day events, so unless you expect to do a lot of this work in your first year I would suggest you keep your insurance costs to the minimum. For more details about your professional and legal liabilities and insurance, see Chapter 4. **Work out your professional and legal costs from Figure 12 below.**

| Professional and legal costs | Annual cost |
|---|---|
| cost of membership of professional bodies | |
| cost of further training and development | |
| cost of keeping first aid certificate up to date | |
| professional insurance | |
| registration fee for Data Protection Act | |
| other | |
| Total | £ |

Figure 12. Professional and legal costs.

### Step 5 – Advertising costs

You will need to set yourself a budget for your advertising costs. The total cost will depend, of course, on where you choose to advertise. As a first-time trader you will usually be able to negotiate cheaper deals with both *Yellow Pages* and *Thomson* directories. If you've decided to advertise via your own website, don't forget to add on the annual costs of hosting the website and the registration of your domain name. The printing costs for any leaflets, brochures and business cards etc should also be added into your budget. For more information about advertising, see Chapter 9. **Work out your advertising costs from Figure 13 below.**

| Advertising costs | Annual cost |
|---|---|
| cost of advertising in *Yellow Pages* or *Thomson* | |
| cost of advertising in local or national newspapers | |
| stationery and print costs for producing leaflets | |
| costs for overprinting any promotional items | |
| website costs | |
| advertising board | |
| other | |
| Total | £ |

Figure 13. Advertising costs.

### Step 6 – Business banking, loans, taxes, NI contributions and accountants' fees

If you decide to use any of the above facilities you are likely to incur some extra charges. Whilst most business bank accounts do not levy charges for the first year of trading for sole traders, you do need to ensure that you make a note of this in your planning for subsequent years (and as a comparator for when you go shopping for business accounts). If you have already enquired about taking out a business or personal loan, you should add into your plan the cost of the monthly repayments (any set up charge will normally be added to the loan).

Although it may be very difficult to have any clear idea of the amount that you are likely to be earning from your business over the first year, you will still need to make an allowance for tax. A rough guide is to allow 20% of your earnings to be set aside for this purpose. *As a self-employed person, you will now be responsible for paying your own National Insurance (NI) contributions,* and you will need to make an allowance for this to be paid from your personal account, not your business account, as this is not a business cost. For further information about NI contributions, see Chapter 12.

Whether you decide to have your accounts reviewed and consolidated each year by an accountant is a matter of your personal choice, as this is not a legal requirement for anyone working as a sole trader. You can, of course, choose to complete your own self-assessment tax return each year. However, many self-employed people find it useful to employ an accountant to go over their books. A good accountant will not only take some of the work off of your shoulders but will usually, through a judicious review of your finances, manage to 'save' you her/his fee. Your accountant can also be called on for business advice. As a general guide, for straightforward bookkeeping and presentation of accounts for a small business, the fees are likely to be in the range of £200–350. **Work out your costs from Figure 14 below.**

| Business banking, loans, taxes, and accountants fees | Annual cost |
|---|---|
| business banking charges (usually waived in the first year – check this) | |
| cost of any personal or business loans | |
| amount set aside for Inland Revenue for tax purposes | |
| accountant's fees | |
| other | |
| Total | £ |

Figure 14. Fees costs.

## Putting together your profit and loss account

Now you've got all the facts and figures at your fingertips, take your planning just one step further. If you find that as a result of this exercise you need to apply to your lender for a loan, you will need to complete a projected profit and loss account for your first year of trading. Even if you find you have no requirement for a loan at this time, it is still a very good idea to complete the final stage of this exercise, as it may help to firm up some of your thinking. Putting your ideas down on paper will help you to clarify your thinking and give you a 'blueprint' to work towards. If you don't have a clear idea of where you want to be with your business in one year's time, you will not have any particular goals to work towards, or measure your success against, or to challenge or cause you to adjust your thinking or direction.

Completing your profit and loss account is not as scary as it might first sound. *You simply need now to work out your projected income for the year*. This is going to be very much a 'guesstimate'. If you have had the benefit of working part-time in a practice you will, of course, have a much clearer idea of your potential earnings. You do need to make allowances for holidays, both bank holidays and personal holidays when you will not be working. And a good general rule for your first year of trading is that you are unlikely to do much more than break even – so work on the basis that because you will be putting a lot of time and energy into setting up and marketing your practice, it is unlikely that you will be able to work and earn at anything more than a quarter of your potential. Therefore, cost out what your potential earnings would be if only a quarter of your client slots were filled each week.

*You will then need to list what your estimated or known expenditure will be for each month*, and then calculate for each month whether you have made a profit or loss (see the table below).

The next step is to *take your total for the year (whether profit or loss) and compare this against your projected total expenditure for your personal living costs* – this will allow you to calculate whether you will need to arrange a loan in order to manage your first year. If you do need a loan, then you should do this exercise again, this time filling in the figures for the next one to two years. If you are going to take out a loan, you should make sure that you have reviewed all your business requirements for the next two to three years in order to cover your costs until such time as you can safely predict that you will be making a reasonable profit.

| Jan | Feb | Mar | Apr | May | June | July | Aug | Sep | Oct | Nov | Dec |
|-----|-----|-----|-----|-----|------|------|-----|-----|-----|-----|-----|
| List your estimated earnings for each month ||||||||||||
| List your estimated or known expenditure for each month broken down into five main headings (take your figures from the tables in the six-step planning process)<br>♦ business premises costs<br>♦ equipment costs<br>♦ professional and legal costs<br>♦ advertising costs<br>♦ business banking, loans, taxes, and accountants fees. ||||||||||||
| *Remember: it is generally easier to average out your expenditure across the months. However, if you know when certain payments are due, for example your professional insurance is always due in February each year, or if you have budgeted for some special expenditure such as a major marketing campaign in a particular month – let your monthly figures reflect these amounts.* ||||||||||||
| Calculate whether you have made a profit or a loss for each month ||||||||||||
| Calculate your overall profit or loss for the year ||||||||||||

If you do need to approach your bank for a loan, your business banking manager will want to see your profit and loss account so be realistic about what you think you can achieve in your first year. Your bank manager will expect you to have put a lot of thought into your planning so be prepared to answer some searching questions about your projected business finances.

> **If you decide to apply for a business bank account, a copy of a profit and loss account is often included in your initial start-up pack – phone around and check what's on offer.**

## Costing the venture

Having completed your first year's financial plan you will now be able to check whether you need to raise some extra money to finance your venture, whether you have sufficient savings to survive the first year or whether you would prefer to work in another occupation part-time in order to offset the costs and generally 'feel' your way. **How would you answer the following questions.**

- How much money will you need in your first year?
- When you will need this money?
- Do you have any savings which you can afford to invest in the practice?
- Do you have insurance plans, PEPs or TESSAs which you could cash in?
- Do you require a loan?
- Do you have any other ways of financing the venture?

### First year financing

Once you know how much money you will need for your first year in practice, you can start to break this down further. Do you need a large injection of cash at the outset in order to fund the set-up costs, or will you be able to afford to start your business by using savings or some of your own personal funds? And whether or not you've managed to fund the initial set-up costs yourself, will you require an extra top-up towards the middle or end of your first year? What does your financial plan reveal?

**If as a result of your planning you know you need to raise some extra cash during your first year in practice, you may want to consider the following:**

- business or personal loans
- grants
- using your savings
- funding from friends and family
- cashing in insurance plans, PEPs, TESSAs
- remortgaging
- using your credit cards.

### Business or personal loans

If you need a loan it's generally best to try your own bank first. You will have built up a credit rating over the time you have banked with that company and your own bank is likely to give any request a sympathetic hearing. If you already have a business bank account, or are thinking of setting one up, check out the differences between the personal versus business banking loan rates. A business bank loan may be more cost effective, it will also help you to keep your business finances separate from your personal accounts and therefore make record keeping slightly easier. Whichever route you choose – do your homework first. **Be realistic about your needs and be prepared to demonstrate how you think your business will progress in that first year.** You will be asked questions about local competition, marketing, set-up costs and working capital – be sure to have your answers ready and be prepared to back these up with your projected profit and loss forecast for the year. If you are offered loan payment protection to help you meet your repayments if you are unable to work due to sickness or injury, check that this protection covers you in your self-employed capacity – this is particularly important if you are taking out a personal loan.

### Grants

Depending on your age, the nature of the business you are engaged in and the area in which you are located, you may be eligible for certain grants. The Prince's Trust offers financial help and support for young people aged 18 to 30 (18 to 25 in Scotland) who are setting up in business. They will not consider certain complementary therapies, such as massage therapy, but they will consider others on a case-by-case basis. The Trust can offer low interest loans of up to £5k. They also offer self-help kits, have free advice lines and can provide you with a mentor for up to three years. For further information about the Prince's Trust, see Chapter 12.

Business Link runs a nationwide scheme offering free advice on setting up your business, which operates at a local level. They can help you write a business plan and sort out your tax and National Insurance contributions. Business Link has an on-line directory which will allow you to see if there are any government grants or schemes which may be available in your local area. For further information about Business Link, see Chapter 12.

If you are treating specific medical disorders and your therapy has a good track record for helping treat those particular medical conditions, then an approach to a relevant medical charity may also bring in some form of help or support. Even if financial help is not on offer, they may hold your details on their database or directory of suitably qualified complementary practitioners – which means you may get some referrals. For further information, see Chapter 12.

Don't forget to check whether the organisations you trained with make any form of grants or awards. These groups could also provide you with a good source of further contacts.

### Using your savings

You may regard this as your preferred option rather than taking out a loan. The advantages are clear – no interest rates, no set-up charges, nothing to pay back. However, you should think carefully before investing some, or all, of your savings in the business. What were the savings originally intended for? How will you, or your family, feel if the money for that longed for foreign holiday or new kitchen is now transformed into business premises or equipment? If you decide to use your savings determine how much you can leave untouched, either for emergencies or to put towards that holiday or dream kitchen. **Maintaining a healthy balance is everything – don't sacrifice all your savings for the sake of your new venture.**

### Funding from friends and family

Although well-meaning friends and family members may be only too happy to offer you some cash towards setting up your practice, this is not without its problems. A lot of friendships break up over money issues, and family rifts are common. That said, **there are advantages in choosing this route**:

◆ minimal or no interest rates being charged
◆ no set-up charges
◆ no penalties for early settlement of the loan.

However, for everyone's peace of mind it is best to have a contract drawn up which details how much has been loaned and by whom, when the loan needs to be paid back, what, if any, interest is to be applied and how the loan is to be paid back, eg £100 a month by standing order to Uncle Bert's personal bank account. It is not necessary to have a solicitor draw up a formal document, but to give it a legal standing do ensure that the agreement is dated, signed by all parties and that an independent party witnesses the signatures. This document should clearly outline all the responsibilities with regard to the loan and therefore should prevent any confusion or disagreements from arising.

### Cashing in insurances and long-term savings plans

Although these clearly provide a means of raising extra cash, just like using your savings, if you choose to cash in on any of your long-term savings plans you should first carefully consider your motivations and priorities. Would it be more beneficial for you to spend your 'nest egg' on that long foreign holiday that you've always been promising yourself rather than just keeping the business buoyant? It could also be a comfort to know that you have some money in reserve so that should the worst happen you can manage financially for a few months while things settle down or you get another job.

In reality, *setting up your own business is not a good time to cash in on any life insurances.* Instead it's a time when you would be better advised to think about increasing any insurances you may have, or combining your insurance in some way with a pension plan – if you haven't already made suitable provision.

### Remortgaging

If you already own property this is another potential source of funds, particularly if you are thinking of working from home and looking to extend or modify your property for this purpose. For example, remortgaging in order to fund the building of a conservatory which can double up as your practice room; knocking down walls to increase the size of a room, building a new wall to section off your new work area; widening doorways to accommodate wheelchair users or building a downstairs toilet to save your clients having to negotiate your stairs. Approached carefully, these modifications could also add to the value of your property as well as making it more comfortable and practical to work from home.

Even if you are not considering working from home, if you haven't changed your mortgage for a number of years you may be pleasantly surprised by the deals that are currently on offer. These could save you money on your current mortgage and therefore allow you that bit extra to put towards your new business.

### Using your credit cards

Credit cards are often overlooked as a form of small short-term loans. It could be that as a result of your financial planning all you will require is a small amount of financial security over the coming months, and therefore the flexibility of a credit card 'loan' which you can use as and when you need to, and which you can pay back in varying amounts, should not be undervalued.

If you don't already have a credit card, now's the time to investigate the options and perhaps take out one or two cards. Alternative therapies, just like other businesses, suffer from cashflow problems from time to time, and having a credit card facility can be a very flexible way of handling this situation creatively and providing a welcome boost to your working capital.

# CHAPTER FOUR

# Insurance, Professional and Legal Requirements

## What legal and professional requirements do I have to meet?

The specific legal and professional requirements you will need to meet will vary according to the type of therapy you practise. However, there are some requirements which will apply to any therapist regardless of the nature of their practice. **You will need:**

- to take out appropriate professional insurance
- to comply with the provisions of the Disability Discrimination Act
- to comply with the provisions of the Data Protection Act
- to comply with any other relevant legislation
- to comply with client confidentiality
- to comply with financial and taxation legal requirements
- to comply with the membership requirements of any professional bodies of which you are a member.

## Insurance

**Wherever you practise, and whatever therapy you are engaged in, you will need to take out appropriate cover for your professional and legal liabilities.**

Most professional bodies will not list your practice in their directory or on their website unless you can prove that you have taken out adequate insurance to cover any professional and legal liabilities you may incur. Your clients are unlikely to ask you whether you are insured, but it is always good practice to confirm your insurance status in your practice brochure and in any fliers or leaflets you may distribute.

**All practising professional therapists should have their own professional indemnity and public liability insurance cover.**

Whether you require any other insurances will depend on the work you are engaged in and where and how you practise. Many professional organisations offer blanket insurance cover as part of their membership fee. And most training schools and institutions effect their own insurance for students whilst they are training, and can offer good deals for graduate students who want to insure with the same company. If you practise more than one therapy you do need to insure that each therapy is adequately covered – if in doubt talk it through with your insurers.

### Professional indemnity insurance

This is a must for any practising therapist, as it covers you for any legal action taken against you as a result of your work or your products. It is unlikely to be an expensive undertaking unless your therapy work has a high risk attached to it. A number of insurers offer low-cost policies which take into account all your professional risks and for a moderate increase in premium will include any other therapies that you practise under the one blanket policy.

Depending on the nature of your work you may have one or more endorsements attached to your policy. These are rarely very limiting, and normally only relate to activities outside the usual bounds for your particular therapy. For example, a Qi Gong practitioner may have an endorsement on their insurance policy which means that they are not covered for giving injections as part of their therapeutic work. This would not affect most Qi Gong practitioners and instructors as their work is non-invasive. However, you do need to check carefully any endorsements that are made to your policy in case these do relate to you and the way in which you work.

You should be thinking in terms of £2 million cover at least. If you are thinking of doing corporate work or hiring rooms for workshops or seminars, you might want to increase your cover to £5 million.

### Public liability insurance

This covers your liabilities at law in respect of anyone who enters your premises as part of your work. For example, if one of your clients has the misfortune to trip over the edge of your carpet, falls and breaks their wrist and can't work, they may decide to sue you for their loss of earnings – this is the kind of accident that this insurance covers. *You may think the likelihood of this happening is remote, but you should insure for this just the same.* If you work in rooms in a shared or managed building, the landlord's public liability insurance will cover any accidents occurring in the common parts of the building such as the toilets or on the stairs, but you will need your own cover for your rooms or workspace.

### Office contents insurance

It is not a professional requirement to insure your office contents, but you should give some thought to whether you could afford to replace all your equipment should the worst happen and you lose it all in a fire, or some of your equipment or furniture gets stolen. If you are working from home, you may well find that most of your equipment is already covered under your household contents policy. However, it is worth checking that any specialist equipment you may be using is also covered, and that the maximum limits on your insurance cover are adequate for both your household and business purposes.

If you are working from rented rooms you will need to take out your own office contents cover. This can be arranged with most insurance companies for a relatively small charge depending on the amount and type of equipment you have. Be prepared to answer questions about existing security precautions, as the insurers will be looking for confirmation that you have limited the risk of any theft by ensuring that windows are lockable, that access to the premises is secure and that there is a burglar alarm system in operation.

> Get into good habits as soon as possible. If you are hiring a room in an existing practice or are working from a rented room in a shared building make sure you lock your door whenever you leave the room. For no matter how good your insurance policy is, it will not cover you if theft occurs while you have left your equipment unattended.

### All risks insurance

This insurance is also not a professional requirement, but it is a sensible option if you and your equipment are often on the move. Even if you usually work from home, but take your laptop and mobile phone with you when you travel for training or to attend meetings, you should check whether those items are covered, and if not, how disruptive it would be to both your business and your finances to have to replace them. *Again, check your household contents insurance policy first to see if you can separately list these items if they are not already covered elsewhere.* Mobile phone companies often offer good insurance deals and it may be more cost effective to take out insurance with the phone company rather than increase the 'all risks' cover on your household policy.

If the other items you need to insure are not already included on your household policy and you have already taken out or intend to take out office contents insurance, it should be a simple matter to extend your cover and list the equipment you regularly transport on a schedule for 'all risks' cover.

> **Please note: having an 'all risks' insurance policy will not cover you for the loss of any equipment which is left unattended – so be extra cautious when unloading equipment from your car and carrying it to a client's home or training venue.**

## Business interruption insurance

This insurance covers your costs should the worst case scenario happen, i.e. you lose all your equipment, case notes and practice room as a result of a tragic event such as a fire. If you haven't given any thought to how you would operate should such a dire circumstance occur, it is always good to do a little planning for this even in your first year of trading. This insurance will cover your costs if you need to hire another room or office to work from while yours is being restored. It will also cover you for any liabilities you might incur regarding the loss of your data and the costs of retrieving or re-entering the data. Whether you decide to take out cover will depend on the nature and scale of your practice – but it's a good exercise to think around this issue even if you decide not to take out specific cover.

> **It's a good discipline to think about how you could carry on working should the worst happen, and to plan around such an eventuality as much as possible. For example, how effective are your duplicate or back-up computer files, and are these safely stored?**

## Equipment breakdown insurance

If certain pieces of your equipment get very heavy usage, you may want to consider taking out the manufacturer's breakdown insurance. Such items could include your computer or laptop, your printer/copier/scanner and your phone/fax machine – really any heavy-use items where the cost of insurance weighed against the likely cost of repair is favourable. This is particularly useful if you are working to a tight budget. Do bear in mind that you are likely to want to replace or upgrade your equipment every three to five years, so your calculations will need to take this into account – and you might find it helpful to add an extra 10 to 20% on to the original cost to allow for price increases or upgrading the equipment.

### Employers liability insurance

You will not require this insurance unless you are employing others to work for you, but if you do employ others this insurance is a legal requirement. An employee is someone you have included on your payroll system and for whom you are liable as an employer for their safety and wellbeing. This therefore does not mean someone who is working in partnership with yourself, or any other self-employed therapist who may cover some of your work and to whom you may make payments, whether this relates to client referrals or to work they have done.

## Disability Discrimination Act

From 1 October 2004 the Goods and Services Provision, Part III of the Disability Discrimination Act (DDA) 1995 comes into force. *This will affect any therapist who is working from premises which are not accessible by disabled people.* Under this Act, *access* will also include access to toilets, car parking and information, and not just the ability to access your practice rooms.

If you take steps to make your service more accessible to people with disabilities, do bear in mind that you are not allowed to offset the costs of any alterations by charging a disabled client more for your services than you would anyone else. This also goes for home visits. If the only way you can provide access to your services to a disabled person is to work with them in their own home instead of your practice, you cannot charge extra for providing this service. For further information on the Disability Discrimination Act and the requirements regarding accessibility to premises, see Chapter 1.

As *access* also includes appropriate access to the information you provide, whether this is your practice brochure, leaflets or your website, you should ensure that you follow the guidelines for accessibility issues. See Chapter 12 for a list of useful contacts.

## Data Protection Act

The Data Protection Act 1998 requires therapists who keep computer-based client records to register with the Information Commissioner. *Failure to register is a criminal offence.* The Act requires the therapist to keep any personal data about individuals in a secure and confidential manner. It also allows a client the right to see the records which have been kept about them. For more information about keeping client records, see Chapter 6; and for contact details see Chapter 12. The current fee for registration is £35 (no VAT).

*BEWARE!* There are a number of individuals who are posing as 'collectors on behalf of data protection', who visit business premises requesting payment for Data Protection Registration; and there are also a number of businesses which send legal-looking letters demanding payment. They generally charge up to £95 + VAT for notification. The Information Commissioner advises that if you are approached by any of these, you do not make any payment and you notify the local police.

## Sexually transmitted diseases, venereal and infectious diseases – the legal situation

There are special legal provisions relating to sexually transmitted diseases, including HIV, which relate to confidentiality and also to treatment. The situation is complex and the general advice is that if you are asked to treat anyone who has a sexually transmitted disease or infectious disease, and you are in doubt as to what the legal position is, you should take further legal advice.

Please note: If you are working with a child under 16 who is suffering from a sexually transmitted disease, this could raise issues regarding child protection.

The Venereal Diseases Act 1917 made it illegal to treat syphilis, gonorrhoea or soft chancre for payment. Therefore any services you provide should be free of charge.

You must also notify the Department of Health if you are aware that one of your clients is suffering from a notifiable disease (the Public Health (Control of Diseases) Act 1984 provides a full list of diseases which must be notified).

If one of your clients presents with an infectious disease they should not be permitted to come into contact with other people, instead you should persuade them to go and see their doctor. The Public Health (Infectious Diseases) Regulations 1988 provides a full list of the diseases deemed to be infectious.

## Treating children – the legal situation

The Children Act 1989 created the concept of parental responsibility. Parental responsibility lasts until a child reaches the age of 18, or marries before that age. The mother of a child always has parental responsibility for her child and the child's biological father automatically has parental responsibility for the child if he is married to the child's mother. If the child's father is not married to the child's mother, he can acquire parental responsibility by agreement with the mother or by court order. Guardians can also acquire parental responsibility by court order.

If you are treating a child under the age of 16 you will need to get consent for the treatment from whoever has parental responsibility for the child. Get them to sign a consent form – an example is listed below – and keep a copy in your records.

### *Sample of a consent form*

I (*name of person with parental responsibility*) give my consent for (*name of therapist*) to treat my child (*name of child*). I also give my consent for (*name of therapist*) to make any appropriate referrals.

Signed (parent or guardian)...................................... Date .............................

Signature of witness............................................. Date .............................

*Sick children* – A person who has parental responsibility for a child but who is neglecting that child's health and welfare is committing a criminal offence if they don't get appropriate medical aid for a child under the age of 16. Alternative or complementary therapy will not be regarded as medical aid. A therapist who treats a sick child in the full knowledge that no doctor has been consulted could be accused of complicity in a criminal offence and be regarded as having liability in civil law if the child suffers harm as a result of a serious illness going undiagnosed.

If you know that the parents are not providing the child with medical care, you should advise the person with parental responsibility to consult a doctor. If you agree to treat the child in the interim, you will also need to get the person with parental responsibility to sign a statement confirming that you have advised them to seek medical help for their child, and keep a copy of this statement in your records.

### Sample of a warning statement

I (*name of person with parental responsibility*) have been advised by (*name of therapist*) that it is a legal requirement that I consult a doctor regarding the health of my child (*name of child*).

Signed (parent or guardian)...................................... Date ............................

Signature of witness............................................ Date ............................

A provision of the Children Act 1989 is the protection of children who are at risk of harm. Harm includes any form of ill treatment, such as emotional or physical neglect as well as direct physical or sexual abuse. If you suspect that a child brought for treatment is at risk, you should report this to the child's doctor or the social services department serving the area in which the child lives. For this reason it is always advisable that when a child is brought for treatment, the person with parental responsibility for the child gives their consent for the child's treatment and also consent for any appropriate referrals, so that should any issues arise, there is no additional problem of breaching confidentiality without consent.

## Treating a woman in childbirth – the legal situation

No matter how much your particular therapy might benefit a mother-to-be, you should be aware that it is an offence for anyone other than a registered midwife to attend a woman in childbirth without medical supervision. It is also an offence for anyone other than a registered nurse to attend a woman who has recently given birth for a ten-day period after the birth.

So, whatever therapy you use, you will need to either teach your client the techniques she might find useful when in labour, provide tapes or CDs that she can listen to without the need for your personal involvement, issue any essential oils or herbal remedies that she might find useful in advance of childbirth, or treat any conditions, fears or problems well in advance of the expected delivery date.

## Treating animals – the legal situation

The law regarding animal treatment has more restrictions than that for the treatment of humans.

### The Veterinary Surgeons Act 1966

This Act prevents anyone who is not a registered veterinary surgeon from practising veterinary surgery. This includes diagnosing animal injuries and illnesses and giving advice on these. The Royal College of Veterinary Surgeons (RCVS) does accept the treatment of animals by some complementary therapies such as healing. See Chapter 12 for contact details.

Before you treat any animals, you must get the owner to confirm that the animal has already been examined by a vet. If not, a vet needs to make a proper assessment of the animal before any complementary treatments can be given. The animal's vet remains in charge of the case at all times, and the therapist must not countermand or obstruct any treatment the animal is already receiving from the vet. The therapist is not allowed to suggest any form of diagnosis or advise on veterinary treatment. However, a therapist can administer first aid to an animal in an emergency.

## Selling remedies, herbs and medicines – the legal situation

This is a rapidly changing area of law, so you will need to keep up-to-date on the current legislation.

It is illegal for a therapist to prescribe or sell remedies, herbs, oils or any supplements unless they have had appropriate training or have a qualification which legally allows them to do so. The law regarding medicines, herbs and remedies is complex and is developing rapidly – anyone who wants to prescribe, administer or sell remedies needs to research, and comply with, the current legislation.

## Client confidentiality

### Your clients' expectations regarding confidentiality

Your clients will expect that any medical or personal details that they share with you are kept confidential. Quite often they will also request that these details are kept in confidence from any medical professionals from whom they may be receiving treatment. This may be because they feel that their doctor or medical practitioner has let them down, or is not listening to them, or may have refused to refer the client on to you for treatment either because of funding difficulties or because they do not believe the therapy to be beneficial. Clients may also want to keep the fact that they are coming to you for treatments from certain family members. Depending on the nature of the work in which you are involved you may at times need to get the client's permission to consult with their doctor.

### Keeping personal information safe

The provisions of the Data Protection Act require you to keep all client records and personal information safe and secure. Any personal data should be physically locked away when not in use, either in a metal filing cabinet or, if the data is held on your computer, password protected and encrypted.

### Sharing personal information

If you need to share any information about a client you must get their prior signed consent in writing. You must be specific regarding who you are going to share this information with, what you are going to share, and for what purposes. If you have reason to transfer a data file this should be encrypted for security reasons.

You should be particularly careful when requesting help or support from an egroup about a client's problem to ensure they cannot be identified in any way – especially as the security provisions for egroups tend to be very poor. Similarly, if you seek advice from your peer group colleagues, or from your supervisor or mentor regarding aspects of a certain client's problems or treatment plan, you should take care not to identify the client.

**The only time you must disclose any personal information about a client is when you are required to do so by law.**

### Raising awareness of your confidentiality policy

The fact that you are bound to treat any personal records in a highly confidential manner may not be apparent to all your clients, so it is good practice to raise awareness of this issue by featuring brief details about your confidentiality policy in your practice brochure, your code of practice and your website. You should also include a statement on all your emails and on your fax header sheets detailing the confidential nature of your work and the request that any inappropriately received faxes or emails are destroyed and you are notified. See Chapter 8 for a suitable form of words.

### Keeping correspondence and telephone calls confidential

Any correspondence you send to your client should be clearly marked 'Private and Confidential', and there should be no business logos or other distinguishing marks on the envelope by which any other person picking up the post could identify your practice. You should check with your client in advance whether you can safely send any correspondence to their home address, and if not, get details of another address which is safe to use as a postal address. Similarly, you should check with your client during their first session which telephone number it is best to contact them on – some clients will only want you to call them on their mobile in order that they can choose whether or not to accept the call depending on their circumstances at the time. If a client does not want anyone else in the household to know about their treatment but can only give the usual house telephone number for contacting them on, you should ensure that your number is withheld should you need to ring them. If the client needs to ring you from home, you can advise them to dial another number after they have spoken to you, in order that your number cannot be picked up by another member of the household dialling last number recall or 1471.

### Young people and confidentiality

Any young person aged 16 or over is considered a 'responsible' person in law and is therefore able to agree their own medical treatment whether this is through their GP, hospital or clinic, or whether this is a complementary or alternative therapy of their choosing. Parents may sometimes put pressure on you to release information about their

16 year-old, or will try to prevent them from having treatments with you. Just remember that your duty of care remains with your client, not their parents. The situation can become even more muddled where the parents are paying for the treatment and may threaten to withhold payment. If this is the case, you will have to decide how to handle this situation if you can't reason this out with the parents. It may be that you decide to continue with the treatments and agree extended, or reduced, payment terms with the client, or you may decide to waive your fees altogether or get your client to 'pay' for their treatment by doing some leaflet distributing or marketing for you.

> **Children under 16 may also be able to request confidentiality depending on their age, maturity and understanding.**

## Trading status, finances and taxation – the legal situation

### *Trading status*

There are three main ways in which people trade:

- sole trader
- partnership
- limited company.

### Sole trader

The positive aspect of this way of trading is that it is the simplest way in which to set yourself up in business, and it allows you to start trading just as soon as you want to. However, you should be aware that as a sole trader you are personally responsible for any money your business owes.

### Partnership

There two main types of partnership. The first is where two or more people jointly run a business, and just like the sole trader situation, all partners are liable for any money that the business owes. The second form of partnership is the limited liability partnership, this is a common option amongst professionals such as doctors or consultants, who run a risk of incurring negligence claims.

**Limited company**

This is somewhat more complicated and can be expensive to set up. The positive aspect of this form of trading is that your liabilities are limited as the business assets are kept separate from your personal assets. You can get further information about setting up a limited company, as well as details regarding your rights and responsibilities as a company director, from Companies House (see Chapter 12 for contact details). You will need the help of a solicitor or an accountant in order to form your limited company.

*Naming your company*

There are certain rules and regulations regarding naming a company. Companies House can advise on the legal requirements, for contact details see Chapter 12. Before you name your company you must be sure that no one else in the same line of business is using that name.

*Registering as self-employed*

> You will need to register as self-employed within the first three months of self-employment otherwise you will be faced with a penalty charge.

To register as self-employed, phone the Inland Revenue with details of the date you started self-employment – and remember to have your NI number handy. You will then be sent an Inland Revenue starter pack, which will outline your obligations and responsibilities as far as taxation is concerned. You will also be sent a form to complete in respect of your future NI contributions. For further information, see Chapter 12.

*Taxation and self-assessment*

> *Paying tax by PAYE* – If you are only working part-time in your practice to begin with and working the rest of the week for an employer, you may be able to have the tax for your self-employed work payable via PAYE. This does depend on how much you are earning, but generally it is a good way of spreading costs and is therefore worthwhile investigating.

Even if you have never completed one before, you will now be responsible for completing a self-assessment tax form each year. The Inland Revenue will need to receive these forms by 30 September each year if you want them to do the tax calculations for you. If however you are calculating your own tax or using an accountant, you will have until 31 January to complete your return and send it to the Inland Revenue. Failure to comply with the 31 January cut-off date will result in an automatic penalty of £100 plus interest charged on any amounts which you owe the IR. So you need to make sure that you highlight this date in your diary. And remember that you can now complete your self-assessment tax return online (see Chapter 12 for the Inland Revenue contact details).

> **Even if you have employed an accountant to go over your books, it still remains your responsibility to validate the accounts.**

The Inland Revenue has a helpline for small businesses, and it is worth giving them a call with any enquiries you might have, for example, what the potential tax offsets are for certain aspects of your business such as professional training or particular pieces of equipment.

> **If you've registered your business as a limited company, you'll need to pay corporation tax on the profits, but you will also have to pay income tax on your earnings as a director.**

### National Insurance contributions

Contrary to popular belief, these do not form part of your business expenses. Therefore you should arrange to have these paid from your personal bank account. If you weren't sent an NI contributions form with your pack of information from the Inland Revenue, you can get one by contacting the Inland Revenue direct. See Chapter 12 for contact details.

## Membership of professional organisations

Whilst there are usually no legal obligations to join any professional associations, if you are a member of a professional organisation related to your therapeutic work this can help you to increase your standing in the public eye and therefore is very much a professional requirement. **There are a number of benefits to be gained from membership:**

◆ you will be listed on their directory for referrals
◆ your details may be listed on their website with a link to your own website
◆ you may be able to get cheaper insurance cover
◆ you may have your details featured in the organisations' block adverts, eg in *Yellow Pages*
◆ your clients will know the code of conduct you are operating under
◆ your clients will also know of any disciplinary process the organisation has effected
◆ you may benefit from receiving a regular newsletter on related topics
◆ some organisations have egroups and/or advice lines which may be of benefit
◆ you have a potential market for any articles, pamphlets or books you may write
◆ you could make approaches to the organisation regarding supervising students
◆ you could also offer your services as a trainer/lecturer or examiner.

Give some careful thought to which organisations you join. It is usual to be a member of more than one association – though I wouldn't suggest joining more than three. Check out what the benefits of joining a particular organisation will be – what are you getting for your money? It may be that in order to practise your particular therapy you have to be a member of a certain organisation – especially if you require a local authority licence or permission to practisae. Your training school will be able to advise you on this.

> Make sure you keep a copy of your membership certificates on open display in your practice – even if your client hasn't asked what groups you are a member of, they are usually reassured to see your certificates and these can help to open up discussion regarding your professional expertise and training.

### Complying with membership requirements

Any professional organisation will have its own rules governing membership. **These can include complying with:**

◆ the need to be adequately insured
◆ the need to complete a set number of hours of continued professional development each year

- the need to comply with the organisation's Code of Conduct
- the organisation's complaints procedure

## NHS provider numbers

You may get patients referred to you by their GP. If the patient's sessions with you are to be paid for out of NHS funds, you will need to be able to supply your NHS provider number in order to get paid. Acquiring a provider number does not confer any endorsement of your practice, or your treatments, by the NHS – you cannot term your practice as 'NHS registered'. If you would like to request an NHS provider number for your practice, see Chapter 12 for contact details.

## BUPA registration

BUPA have now limited their registration scheme and it is less likely that you will be able to work as a complementary therapist within the BUPA scheme as registration is required before any referrals will be made to you. For further details and to check out whether your complementary therapy can be registered, see Chapter 12.

## What other legal and professional requirements might I have to comply with?

This will, of course, depend entirely on the nature of the therapeutic work which you do. The following list details the most likely additional legislative requirements that you may need to comply with:

- the Health and Safety Act
- various licences and permissions
- any by-laws and Acts specific to your region or location
- local authority inspections
- planning permission.

### Health and Safety Act

This Act governs the health and safety of people in the workplace and some of these regulations may apply to your particular therapy. For example, anyone thinking of setting up as a massage therapist would be well advised to check out the requirements for their practice under the Health and Safety legislation. The premises that any massage therapist works from will need to comply with certain legal requirements, such as the need for washable walls and floors so that any oil spillages can be effectively dealt with.

In any case it is good practice to ensure that your working environment is always clean and tidy, and that any potential hazards such as trailing cables are kept away from walkways or are suitably covered. Other hazards could be things such as too low a level of lighting or worn or frayed carpets. It's your responsibility to ensure that these problems are dealt with.

If you work from rented space in a shared office block or within an existing clinic or practice, you should further ensure both your clients' and your own safety by reporting any potential hazards to your landlord, managing agent or practice manager. Make sure that the fire alarms or smoke alarms are regularly checked, that the number and type of fire extinguishers are adequate and are maintained annually, and also that the fire exits are not blocked in any way or are locked (a very common practice).

> Make sure any health and safety issues are reported to the person in charge. Don't be complacent for it could be your life at risk here as well as that of your clients.

If you are working from home and would find it helpful to have a Health and Safety inspection carried out on your premises, contact your local authority for further help and advice and to arrange an inspection. The Health and Safety Executive offers a national general enquiry service, their contact details are listed in Chapter 12.

### Licences and permissions

Depending on the nature of your work, you may need to apply to your local authority for a licence in order to set up your practice. For further information, and to check out the licensing requirements which may apply to your practice, give your local authority a call (Environmental Health or Consumer Protection Division). An alternative is to contact your local Citizens Advice Bureau (CAB), which will have a list of complementary and alternative therapies and will detail those which require licences or permission to practise.

### Location specific Acts

A good example of this is the requirement for massage therapists in London to comply with the London Local Authority Act 1991 – Special Treatment Premises. This requires that the premises the massage therapist is working from comply with current Health and Safety legislation, and allows for the registration of the premises with the local authority as a bona fide massage therapy establishment, i.e. it is not being operated as a cover for prostitution. It may be possible to be granted some exemptions from the provisions of this Act, for example, if you operate as a travelling masseuse (section 4 b ii). For further information, massage therapists in London should contact the Special Treatment Licences Section of their local authority.

### Local authority (LA) inspections

If your therapy is one which requires licensing by the local authority or permission to practise, it is likely that your premises will be inspected before any licence or permission is granted. The inspection is simply to satisfy the local authority that your premises and practice meet their requirements under the Health and Safety legislation and any other specific legislation. If any alterations or improvements need to be made you will be notified of these and given a time limit in which to carry out the necessary work. There will then be a further inspection before the licence or permission is granted in order for the local authority to validate any changes that have been made.

You should also notify the LA of any major changes that you make to your premises in order that these can be inspected and passed.

### Planning permission

If you are working from home you may need planning permission for your practice. Contact your local authority for further information or for an assessment.

---

**Keep up to date on the regulations affecting your practice.**
Different regulations are coming into effect all the time. Some regulations may require you to belong to a particular organisation or professional body before a licence will be granted, so it is worthwhile checking which organisations are accredited before you join. For some therapies there may also be a need to register with the Health and Safety Executive.

# Publishing a code of conduct for your practice

A code of conduct is a non-leglislative but highly important document which details what your client can expect from you as a professional.

It is very useful to have your own code of conduct (sometimes called a code of ethics or a code of practice) which details for the client the professional conduct to be expected from your practice, the standards you work to and affirms the ethics of your practice. Publishing your code of conduct not only presents you as highly professional, but if you are truly serious about your practice you will want to be setting the standards you work to and this is one way of compiling your own set of competencies.

If you are already a member of a professional organisation you most likely are working to their existing codes, so you might find it helpful to review these and take from them what is useful to your practice and then add your own extras. Don't forget to review the codes of conduct from other organisations as well as these may help you to formulate your own version.

**Any code of conduct should include some or all of the following:**

- a definition of the therapy you are using, how it works and basic details regarding what a client can expect to experience in a session
- the standards to be expected
- details of how and when you may be working with other agencies, eg medical personnel
- any legislation that you must conform to
- your equalities statement.

### *Define your therapy*

Briefly describe the therapy, for example the National Federation of Spiritual Healers (NFSH) describes spiritual healing in their code of conduct as:

> *restoring the balance of body, mind and spirit of the recipient. It is a natural, non-invasive, holistic approach that has the intention of promoting self-healing, to bring a sense of well-being and peace to the recipient.*

Give brief details of how it works, and basic details regarding what a client can expect to experience in a session. For example, the NFSH details 'Contact Healing' as:

> *spiritual healing carried out in the presence of the recipient who may be seated or lying in a horizontal position. The healer may lay hands on the recipient or the hands may be held off the body.*

### Set your standards

**The standards can relate to as many aspects of your work as you want them to, for example:**

◆ the practice environment
◆ your relationship with the client
◆ your relationship with yourself
◆ permissible behaviours
◆ confidentiality
◆ your records
◆ your payment policy
◆ details of your insurance
◆ confirmation of compliance with both local authority and national regulations
◆ complaint procedure
◆ client participation in research
◆ your qualifications
◆ your membership of any professional organisations and their contact details

**Practice environment**

In this part of the code you can state that you will always maintain your practice environment to a high standard, both in terms of equipment and cleanliness, and also in terms of the general atmosphere – effectively ensuring the best possible working environment.

**Your relationship with the client**

Your working relationship with the client could include facts such as that you will always explain or describe your processes to the client before you commence a treatment, and the client should feel free to ask any questions about their treatment or the processes involved which will be answered honestly. Some codes also include the detail that the therapist will not enter into any kind of relationship with the client apart from the required working relationship.

### Your relationship with yourself

This section could include details regarding how you will make every effort to ensure that you are fit to practise and healthy. That you actively recognise your own limits – physically, mentally, emotionally and spiritually, and any training or experience limits. You can qualify this by saying that you will not practise if your own limits have been exceeded, and that as far as training goes you will actively seek further training and experiences so that your skill base is constantly added to. You might even like to detail any regular supervision you undergo and/or any commitment you have made to a minimum level of continued professional development each year.

### Permissible behaviours

Here you could include a statement to the effect that your behaviour will not include any action which could be construed as indecent assault or harassment. And where the client is concerned you could set out that you will not treat anyone who is under the influence of drink or drugs, for example, or who presents as unstable, aggressive or threatening in their manner. You could further list whether or not your client will be expected to remove any clothing, and if so, what items and what arrangements you have made for their privacy. If you touch the client during your work you could also list what this will involve, for example, gentle massage of the neck and shoulders to assist relaxation.

### Confidentiality

Confirm that you will not disclose any personal information gathered during the session without the client's written consent, unless required to do so by law.

### Your records

State that you will keep clear records of any sessions, which will be stored in a safe and secure manner, and will not be disclosed to anyone other than the individual concerned. You could also confirm that your record keeping complies with the Data Protection Act, and that you are registered under the Act, if this is appropriate.

### Payment policy

This could also include your cancellation policy. You should detail how payment can be made, for example, cash or cheque or credit card. You should also confirm whether a client needs to pay for each session as they are treated, or whether they need to pay for a block of treatment in advance. It helps if you can set out your fees structure. If you offer discounts or free initial consultations you should also list these and the qualifying factors, for example, evidence of low income for discounts; free initial sessions only last 30 minutes etc.

### Insurance details

You should list the insurance cover you have in respect of your practice and confirm how the client can view a copy of your insurance certificate – for example, you could state that it is on prominent display in your office.

### Compliance with local authority and national regulations

Wherever you are working from, you should be able to confirm that your practice complies with local authority regulations, and national legislation such as the Disability Discrimination Act.

### Complaint procedure

You should state that you will respond to any criticisms and complaints promptly and constructively. You should offer some guidelines as to how quickly you will respond to a complaint (this can depend on the method used to present it, for example, you may decide that you can respond to a telephoned complaint the same day, but within three days for a written response to a complaint received in writing). You could also refer the client to the section on professional membership and confirm that as a nature of your membership of these bodies you are subject to their complaints procedure. You might like to present highlights of the set procedure or you could refer the client on to the organisation direct to request a copy.

### Client participation in research

If you are going to use any client sessions for research purposes you should set out what this means i.e. that the client will not be able to be identified from the research findings, that written and signed permission will be sought from the client prior to any research being carried out, that you will be following the guidelines of 'XYZ' organisation or research methodology (a copy of which you can provide to the client), that you will make clear to the client the nature and purpose of the research.

*Please note* – if you intend to use some of your client data for research purposes you may need to register under the Data Protection Act. For more information, see Chapter 12.

## Qualifications

Here you can state your qualifications and the training you have received. Confirm any titles you are entitled to use, and any abbreviations you are entitled to use after your name – explain what they stand for.

## Professional membership

You should list your membership of any professional organisations, state the level of your membership, confirm any abbreviations you are entitled to use after your name and give the contact details for each organisation in order that your client can check your credentials should they so wish.

## *Working with other professionals*

You should include a short statement detailing how you will work with other health care professionals. This could include stating that you recognise the following:

♦ My service is not an alternative to orthodox medical advice.

♦ I am aware of and respect the rights of other health practitioners.

♦ If appropriate I will ask a client if they have seen a doctor concerning their condition, and if not, advise them to do so.

♦ I accept that if a doctor refers a patient to me, the doctor remains clinically responsible for the patient.

♦ If a doctor refers a patient to me, I will keep the doctor informed of progress.

♦ I will not countermand or obstruct any treatments prescribed by a doctor.

♦ If I am asked to work with a patient in hospital, I will obtain the permission of the ward manager before working with the patient.

## *Legislation*

List whatever legislation is applicable to your practice, and then confirm as appropriate –

that you are either working within the legal guidelines, or that you fulfil the legal criteria, or that you comply with the legislation.

### Your equalities statement

You need to tailor this to fit your own requirements but your statement could be something along these lines:

> *I will always treat my clients in a caring and non-judgmental way, treating everyone appropriately and fairly according to their needs and regardless of issues such as race, class, age, gender, background, disabilities, religion, marital status or sexual orientation.*

# CHAPTER FIVE

# Money Matters

## Banking

Now that you running your own business you will need to keep accurate and verifiable financial records. One of the first things you will need to do is to decide how you are going to keep your personal accounts separate from your business finances, whether this is by opening a business bank account or a second personal bank account.

## Do I need a separate business bank account?

A bank account for your business is going to be one of the first things that you need to set up, and contrary to popular belief you do not necessarily need to have a business bank account.

Therapists who go into business with 'sole trader' status (which means that they are personally liable for any money owed to the business), do not have to have a business bank account if they are trading in their own name. Instead, it is permissible to use an existing personal bank account or set up a designated second account to operate as the 'business' account. However, if you are setting up in business as a limited company you will need to open a business bank account.

## Why might I find a business bank account useful?

Even if there is no legal requirement for you to have a business bank account, it does make good financial sense to check out what benefits you might get from having a business account, and compare these to the cost of running such an account.

**The usual benefits of business banking are:**

- it is easier to keep your business and personal financial records separate
- it appears more professional to have a business account
- you will have access to the support of a business manager who knows your business
- you may have access to cheap deals such as website construction
- you will usually have access to a business support or egroup
- interest is now often paid on business accounts
- it will make it easier for you to get a bank loan for your business
- you will get a fast response to any enquiries
- there will be a higher degree of security in respect of your account
- you will get a variety of ways of banking: in person, over the phone, on the internet.

Some banks may also offer you free book-keeping systems or software, free entry in certain directories or websites, free business guides and free connection to your own freephone number. Others may offer you free business banking depending on the way in which you run your account.

**It is worth shopping around to see what deals are on offer!**

### Setting your service levels

With some banks you can choose the type of working relationship that you want to have with your business manager. Given the average turnover for most therapists, it is unlikely that you will require a high degree of input from your business manager, especially if you are operating as a sole trader. If the only advice you are likely to require is regarding business loans or other common financial transactions, you can keep your costs to a minimum by opting for the lowest level of support – this will generally be phone advice rather than face-to-face meetings. This level of service and support is usually provided free of charge.

### Discounted banking

Most business bank accounts stagger the charges that are applied to your day-to-day transactions for at least the first two years. Quite often you will not be charged anything for any payments into, or withdrawals from your account during your first year of trading (please note – this does not include the set-up fees should you decide to take out a business loan). In subsequent years reduced discounts may apply, for example a 50% discount for your second year of trading and a 25% discount for your third year. This may mean for some accounts that it's not until year four, by which time you should be fully set up and running, that you will incur the full charges.

### Getting a good deal for your money

If you set your business banking service levels at a low level, you are already saving on your business banking costs. Taking advantage of any discounted charges will also help to minimise your costs during your first year of trading. **Other ways in which you keep your costs to a minimum are:**

♦ maintaining your account over the internet, or by telephone
♦ limiting the number of times you pay into your account
♦ limiting the number of times you make a withdrawal from your account
♦ accepting cheques as payment only if the value exceeds a certain amount
♦ using any cash you are paid to pay your business bills
♦ paying your bills by the cheapest method, eg direct debits rather than cheques.

### Keeping down the costs of business banking

Generally, the cheapest way to run your business account is by operating it over the internet, or by telephone or telebanking. This means you will have no face-to-face contact with your business manager apart from the initial set-up interview. *Operating your account in this way means that you only pay for the transactions you carry out* – that is paying money and cheques in, drawing money out and for any direct debits or standing orders you may have set up on your account. Different charges are made for different types of transactions, so if you have regular payments to make, for example paying the office rent or paying invoices for supplies, it's worth checking out the cost of setting up direct debits rather than electronic transfers, and paying over the phone by business debit card compared to the cost of issuing a cheque. Also, as you are charged each time you pay money into a business account it is worthwhile having a regular routine for payment, for example once a week.

### Further good financial practice

It is best to get into a good routine regarding your finances and banking procedures right from the start. **It often helps to allocate a specific day each week for:**

- paying any money into your account
- paying any bills which you are going to pay in cash
- reviewing your statements
- checking your cash flow
- entering all your receipts into your system
- updating your spreadsheet or your manual records.

**At the end of each month:**

- take an overview of your financial situation
- complete your monthly totals on your spreadsheet or manual records
- decide on your takings for that month and transfer the money into your personal account
- calculate (roughly) how much you need to set aside for tax
- transfer the money for your tax bill into your business savings account
- decide how much money you need to leave in the account as a 'float'
- sweep any extra monies across into your savings account.

## Savings accounts

As well as your business account you should think about setting up a savings account for the business. Whilst it might seem unlikely that you are going to have much in the way of savings in your first year of trading, you will need to ensure that you have money put aside to pay your tax bill at the very least. *In the same way that it is often easier to separate out your business and personal finances by holding separate accounts, so it is with any monies that you wish to allocate for a particular purpose.*

If you are working as a sole trader you do not need to set up a business savings account, but can instead set up a second savings account with your existing personal savings account bank or building society. You may even be able to take advantage of the generally higher interest rates available with an on-line savings account – but do read the small print first as most will not allow you to transfer funds to and from a business account or to pay in cash, which means that you may need to be creative in moving your money around between your business and personal accounts. Again the important thing is to keep your personal and business savings separate, so that your accounts can clearly reflect your business savings.

## Loans

For your first year of trading, any loans that you may require should have been considered as part of your original set up costs (see Chapter 3). If your budgeting and planning have been effective in subsequent years, you should have some money set aside to fund, at least in part, any major purchases. However, there may come a time when you have some unexpected big purchase to make, or have decided that the environment is just right for that big business expansion ahead of your planned time.

You should have no trouble getting a business loan if you can prove that your purchase is essential for the running of your business, that you have researched thoroughly all the aspects of your proposed business expansion and can provide a detailed and costed plan of your proposals – and your financial situation is economically viable. A lot will depend on the amount you are requesting, the period of time you require to pay it back and the financial 'health' of your business – remember your business manager will have all your details at their fingertips.

> If you think you may require business loans for your practice, make sure you check out the business loan rates that are being charged before you decide which company you wish to bank with.

If you encounter any problems with getting your business loan, it may be in your best interests to shop around to see if any other lender will make you the loan – even if this means changing banks, as some lenders will accept higher risks than others.

## Credit cards

**You may want to consider using a separate credit card for your business, for example:**

- if you are often on the move with a mobile practice
- if you spend time touring the country, perhaps training at different venues
- to help smooth over any cash flow crises.

You can either apply for a business credit card to run in conjunction with your business bank account, or take advantage of some of the good deals that are currently available on the internet for accounts which you operate via the internet. Accounts operated via the internet will make you responsible for printing out your statement on a monthly basis, as the credit card company usually saves on its costs by pushing the paperwork onto the consumer. However, this does generally result in a lower annual percentage rate (APR) than most other conventional credit cards. Some companies offer flexible packages where you can create your own mix of benefits, for example, you can have an even lower APR on your card if you decide not to receive cash back benefits from purchases made using the card (generally around 0.5% of sales paid back to the consumer in some form), and by agreeing to pay the minimum amount due each month by direct debit.

If you know that because of potential cash flow problems there will be times when you will be using your credit card heavily, it's a good idea to take out a second card with another company in order that you can take advantage of any 0% balance transfers by shifting the debt across from one card to the other.

## Keeping your accounts

It is essential that you keep all your financial records in order that you can verify your accounts should you be required to do so, and also in order that you can complete your self-assessment tax form.

### The need for routine

If you get into good record-keeping habits right at the start it will save you a lot of time. If you get into the habit, as suggested previously, of allocating a set day day each week for your banking transactions and record keeping, it will be a simple matter to extend this principle to include keeping *all* your financial records up to date. If you have a particular day allocated to this task you are less likely to forget to do it thereby allowing a backlog to build up.

### What records do I need to keep?

**You will need to keep copies of the following:**

- client payment receipts
- any other receipts for payments made to the business
- any invoices – whether generated by yourself or from other companies
- receipts for any purchases
- receipts for any transport costs incurred
- receipts for any training you have undertaken
- your business bank statements
- your personal bank statements
- any credit card statements related to business expenses
- any bills for rent or utilities
- phone bills, including mobile phone bills and any internet charges
- cheque stubs
- paying-in book stubs or counterfoils.

### *How should I keep these records?*

Whatever method you choose to keep these records, whether you use a spreadsheet package or enter the details manually, it is often easier to keep a record of the income and expenditure you have incurred on a daily basis.

Even if you choose to utilise a spreadsheet for your accounts you will need to keep paper copies of all your other records. These are best stored in plastic wallets within a box file. This way you can keep all your income details and receipts for each month in a separate plastic wallet to your expenditure details and receipts. Label the plastic wallets accordingly (month and income or expenditure) and then it will be a simple matter for yourself or your accountant to check back and confirm any details.

### Keeping manual records

This is an easy and cheap way of keeping your accounts. You can use a diary to record any financial transactions on a daily basis, and sum up the totals at the end of each week as well as at the end of the month. The Inland Revenue produces a Tax Tracker diary which you may find helpful as it has a useful layout, contains additional tax information and reminds you of the all-important dates you need to comply with for your tax return. You can get a copy of the Tax Tracker diary from any good stationers.

In addition to keeping a diary, you may find it useful to print off a sheet detailing your finances under their various headings, **an example is given on page 92 (Figure 15) which you can amend to reflect your business needs. You can also use this sheet for either your**

**weekly or monthly figures.** Setting your accounts out in this way will help you to summarise your spending under the various categories, and enable you to see at any stage just how much you are spending on any one category. You can then check these figures against your scheduled monthly budget to see if your budget is keeping in line with your spending.

Make sure you keep your financial records locked away in your filing cabinet when you are not working on them.

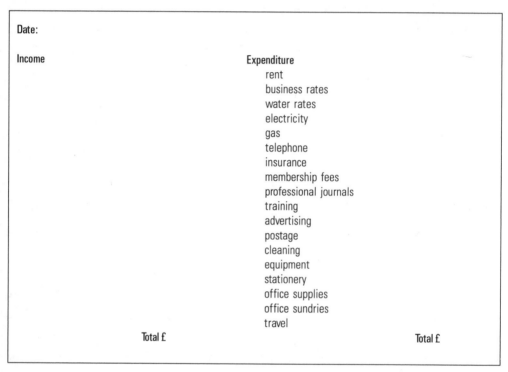

Figure 15. Sample financial record sheet.

**Keeping computer records**

Instead of keeping manual records you may choose to use the spreadsheet package that came with your computer software, or a package that your bank may have sent you when you opened your business account. The advantage of using a spreadsheet package is that the figures are automatically calculated which can save you time. If you choose to keep your records this way make sure you print off your monthly figures at the end of the month to add to your paper records – and equally important, make sure you back up your files. Also ensure that you keep your financial records safe by password protecting entry into your system and encrypting the files.

## Making use of 'quiet' times

When you have spent some time working in your practice you will get a clearer idea of what the usual 'quiet' times are. These are the times when there are fewer clients seeking sessions with you. For some therapies this is during the summer months when the children break up from school and people are taking their holidays. If you find this to be the case for your practice, then you can use this time for gathering all your accounts together and starting work on completing your self-assessment tax form. If you are filing your accounts without the aid of an accountant you may find this quiet period in the year extremely valuable as it will allow you to complete your form before the 30 September deadline – which means that the Inland Revenue will calculate your tax for you.

## Using an accountant

You can choose whether or not to use an accountant to review your books and compile your self-assessment tax return. There is no legal requirement for a sole trader to use an accountant's services.

> **Whether or not you use an accountant, you are ultimately responsible for validating any financial returns.**

**The benefits of using an accountant are:**

- They will often be able to save you the cost of their fee by a careful review of your finances.

- You have another professional to draw on for advice in relation to your business.

- Your accountant can organise your accounts for you if you don't have the time or are unable to organise them yourself – an extra charge will be made for this.

Many people rely on personal recommendations from their colleagues, friends or family in order to find an accountant. You can find an accountant by checking out the listings in your local *Yellow Pages*. It's always worth contacting a few to see which one you feel more comfortable with, for example, you may want an accountant who has worked on the financial records of other therapists and therefore understands more about your business, or you may prefer to use an accountant who will visit you in your own offices to save time and save transporting your files.

If possible, choose a firm of accountants rather than someone working on their own, this way you will be able to tap into additional expertise should the need arise, and there will always be someone around to cover for holidays and sickness – and it doesn't necessarily mean you will have a larger fee to pay.

## Income

In your practice brochure you should confirm how you can accept payment, whether this is in cash, by cheque (with cheque guarantee card) or via debit or credit card, in order to save any payment problems when the client attends for their session. Generally speaking, the more ways in which a client can pay you, the better.

### Accepting payment by cheque or cash

You must at the very least be able to accept payments by both cheque and cash. If your client is paying by cheque make sure they date and sign the cheque correctly, and make a note on the back of the cheque of the number on their cheque guarantee card – this ensures that you will receive payment.

### Post-dated cheques

You will need to decide on your own policy regarding whether or not you accept post-dated cheques. Accepting a post-dated cheque can sometimes be helpful to the client and allow them to afford your session as they may need to wait until the end of the month until their bank account can support the cheque. You may choose to decide this on an individual basis depending on the rapport you have with the client, or how many sessions they have already had with you and their personal needs.

Another time when you may find it helpful to accept a post-dated cheque is when a client is paying for a place on one of your training courses, where they want to confirm the place but can't afford to release the money until nearer the time. Other ways in which I've accepted these is as payment for a block of work or training, where the individual cannot afford the full cost at the time but is prepared to issue say six post-dated cheques already filled out one for each month until the bill has been paid.

### Accepting payment by debit or credit cards

If you can accept payment by debit or credit cards so much the better. Payment by credit card is the only way some clients can afford to pay for their treatments, for others it makes payment more of a convenience as fewer people these days seem to carry their cheque books with them. Each credit card transaction will cost you a certain percentage of that transaction. It will usually involve you in the cost of a machine so that you can take an imprint of the card – you may also need to call a credit agency in order to confirm that the amount will clear successfully.

Another way in which you can accept credit card payments is through internet systems such as PayPal. In order to be able to do this both you and your client need to have internet access. You will both need to set up PayPal accounts, which will require you to enter your credit card details. $1 (US) will then be taken from your accounts in order to test that the transactions work and that the accounts are valid. This can be a somewhat laborious process for a client to go through if they are simply trying to pay you for their session, but it is a very useful way of getting payment for any products you may be selling via your website as foreign currencies are converted into pounds sterling and debited and credited accordingly. For more information about the PayPal system, see Chapter 12.

### Paying small amounts by cheque or credit card

Depending on the charges you make for your sessions you may decide to have a policy regarding the minimum amount you will accept from a client by cheque or credit card. This is purely for practical reasons, as you will be charged on your business account for each cheque you present for payment, and also charged for each credit card transaction you process.

## Tax credits and grants

If you have children under the age of 16, you may be eligible for an increased amount of Child Tax Credit and Working Tax Credit if your income falls below a certain level. And depending on the area in which you live, other payments may be made even if your child is over 16 years of age. For example, in some areas students aged 16–18 are eligible for Education Maintenance Grants of up to £30 per week depending on parental income. Please note the period against which your income is assessed is the previous financial year, as these awards are always assessed retrospectively. Check this out with your local education authority. For further information on tax credits, see Chapter 12.

## Pensions and health plans

Now is a good time to give some thought to making provision for your long-term future. If you were previously in a company pension scheme before taking the self-employed route, you should consult with the company on what the possibilities are where your pension is concerned.

**If you are setting a pension up from scratch or taking out an additional pension, it pays to shop around.**

Check out the deals available through your bank or building society, and also check out the big-name companies. *Whatever plan you go for, it needs to be both affordable and realistic in terms of how you want to be provided for when you decide to retire.* If you are bringing up a young family you might also want to compare what each company offers in terms of death benefits.

If you decide, because of the cost of initially setting up your practice, that you want to leave any payments to your pension fund on hold for a year or two, do make sure that it is for just that year or so as many people fail to make adequate provision for their retirement, and for their families.

The government has a good website offering impartial advice on pensions, see Chapter 12 for further details.

An independent financial adviser will also be able to advise you on pension plans which combine a pension with life insurance cover. They will be able to review your overall financial position, advise you on how best to utilise your finances and help you to think creatively around the financing of your practice and your long-term goals. For further information about independent financial advisers, see Chapter 12.

## Insurance

Now is also a good time to review your personal insurance cover.

### *Life insurance*

Are your life insurance policies adequate, especially now you have your own business? Could you benefit from rearranging cover? If money is tight, you might benefit by transferring to a lower cost scheme. Shop around for the best deals. This is another area that you might want to investigate with an independent financial adviser.

### *Health and sickness insurance*

In addition, you might like to consider augmenting your cover by taking out additional health cover. As you are now self-employed, you will need to make some provision should you be off sick from work for any length of time.

### *Endowments*

If you've been advised that your endowment policy is not performing as well as hoped, and particularly if this is linked to paying back some or all of your mortgage, you should be taking action now. Contact your endowment company for further advice and details of the possible options you could take.

## Making your will

If you haven't already done so, get this sorted now, especially if you have a young family, have business premises, or business interests to take into account. If you have already made a will, review it in light of your new business venture in case any alterations need to be made. *It is also worthwhile making a note to review your provisions every three to five years to check that they still reflect the current situation.*

Any solicitor can assist you in drawing up a will.

## Other sources of income

There are a number of ways in which you can add to, or maximise, your income from your practice. Some of these will require you to have developed your techniques and to have worked in your chosen therapy for a reasonable length of time in order that you can bring sufficient experience to your role. **Some are based more on teaching and research:**

◆ teaching – both members of the public and therapy students
◆ mentoring
◆ writing articles or books
◆ producing training manuals
◆ examining
◆ lecturing.

If you would like more information on these topics, see Chapter 7.

**Other methods of generating more income will cause you to branch out in new ways:**

◆ corporate work, or corporate health awareness days
◆ selling own brand products, eg tapes, oils etc
◆ working flexibly, eg offering phone and email consultations, teleconferencing
◆ hiring out your room to others
◆ keeping your costs down by regular review.

### Corporate work

> If you aren't already working within the corporate sector then you should explore the possibilities of doing so, as the benefits are not just financial (you can charge a corporate rate for your services) – you can gain some helpful publicity for your practice and it gives you a chance to network.

Some organisations have therapists working regularly within the company, others may be new to the idea. If you are looking to work within the corporate sector as an addition to your practice elsewhere, you can work in a peripatetic role. And if you are only visiting the company for an hour or two each week it may be easier for you to be allocated some space and an appropriate slot.

Do think carefully about how you can maximise your time, as this will also help you in your approach to the company. For example, if you are teaching yoga or t'ai chi , emphasise their relaxation benefits and the fact that you can work with a number (state how many) of people in each class or session. And be open to offering early morning, after work or lunchtime sessions. The company may decide to pay you for your services direct, in which case you will need to have given some advance thought to what you are going to charge as your corporate rate, or they may simply provide the space and you will need to collect payment from the staff members attending your sessions.

### Selling your own products

All kinds of products get sold by therapists. For example:

- herbal remedies
- relaxation tapes or CDs
- self-help manuals
- essential oils
- equipment, such as made-to-order massage couches.

These are all sources of generating passive income, which are important in their own right as well as for their ability to help you over any lean times. If your products sell well, then you might want to consider producing and marketing some of your range in a more professional way, for example, getting your relaxation CDs recorded professionally or seeking retail outlets for your products. You will need to ensure that you have appropriate professional insurance cover and that you comply with any legislation concerning your products.

### Working flexibly

Many life coaches have based their practice on telephone, fax or email contact rather than face-to-face consultations, and it's worth exploring whether your practice could benefit from this extremely flexible way of working. The good news for the clients are the savings they can make in respect of both time and money. If your sessions can be conducted over the phone, your client will not have to spend time travelling to you for a session, and they can potentially fit the session in around their work or any home commitments much more easily. And, of course, it means that both of you can work from any location without distance being a barrier.

Some therapists who work in this way specialise in very short sessions with the client – not more than 30 minutes, and request that the client pay for a block of time in advance and deduct the session times as they are used. It tends to be therapists who are involved in 'talking' therapies who can make the best use of this method. However, you could adapt this to other parts of your work, for example, you could let a phone or email consultation take the place of your usual free initial face-to-face consultation.

*Working in this way may involve you in acquiring some different skills.* Some therapists find it hard to move from face-to-face contact to advising over the phone. A possible way of getting round this problem is to invest in a webcam package so that you still see the client and their responses while you talk to them – though this does depend on the client having a similar set-up.

This way of working tends to appeal to people in the business sector who would otherwise find it hard to get the time to work with you on a personal level – so this is another way in which you could market your services.

### Hiring out your room to others

If you have any space during your working week in which your practice rooms are idle, you might want to consider sharing your practice with another therapist in order to gain some extra income. The therapist with whom you share doesn't necessarily have to offer the same therapy, in fact it can be to your advantage to have different therapies operating from the same rooms as this can help to build your practice as the two of you may cross refer. At the very least it means more people become aware of your practice.

There are some key points to bear in mind. **You will need to:**

◆ be clear about the days and times your sharer can work in the practice
◆ treat this arrangement as a formal business contract
◆ agree whether you will share the advertising in any way
◆ agree how you will charge for the room – for example an hourly rate or splitting the costs on a percentage basis
◆ consider whether the sharer will be able to use your rooms if you are away on holiday
◆ check that your practice complies with all the necessary regulations for the additional therapy
◆ agree whether you will have separate contact telephone and email addresses, or whether you will share the responsibility for handling bookings

- consider what other equipment may be required, whether there is space for this and where it will be stored
- check that the other therapist is insured, suitably qualified and has their own code of conduct
- be able to trust the other therapist to lock up and keep your property and premises safe and secure
- consider a trial period in order to test that the arrangement is workable.

You will also need to check that such an arrangement is allowed under the terms of your lease or occupation of the property, agree a minimum hire period (renewable), and issue a receipt or invoice for each booking period.

### Keeping your costs down

This is an often overlooked way of increasing your income by reducing your expenditure, which many businesses forget to review. If you are keeping your monthly financial records up to date you will be able to work out just what percentage of your income is spent on various bills. If, for example, you are grossing £500 per week, but the rent for your room is £200 per week, you are effectively working for two days each week before you have even met the cost of your rent. Once you start looking critically at your finances you may be able to pick out other trends, for example spending 10% of your income each month on phone and internet bills.

Hopefully this should start you thinking about whether these high amounts of expenditure on certain items are in your best interests, and if not, what you could do to change them. If rent bills are a problem you could perhaps get someone to share your room, look for a smaller and cheaper room in the same block, or think about moving the practice into your home. With phone and internet bills, review how you are using this equipment (time of day and length of time), cut down where you can and compare the packages on offer from other phone and internet service provider, to see if you can get a better deal.

*Even if you just make a saving of £10 per week, over a year that's enough for a short holiday or maybe you could put it towards some equipment you've been promising yourself.* When things get tough financially, you should look to cutting existing costs first before you make any major adjustments to the way you work.

# CHAPTER SIX

# Keeping Records

## Why keep records?

Whatever therapy you practise, you will need to keep clear and accurate records of your activities for financial, professional and legal reasons.

## What records do I need to keep?

- client records
- financial records
- training records and certificates
- insurance records and certificates
- professional membership records and certificates.

## Client records

### Client case history sheets

You will need to devise your own best way of keeping your client records. Most therapists use some form of pre-printed client case history sheet or a computer-based equivalent. This document will act as a complete record of the client's contact, personal and medical details, and will be used to detail the treatment that the client receives each time they attend for a session – see the example on page 103 (Figure 16).

You may need to include further details on your client case history sheet, but this will depend on the work you are engaged in and the need to comply with any legal, insurance or professional requirements related to your practice.

---

Sample client case history sheet

Name:
Address:


Telephone nos: Home                     Work                    Mobile
Email address:
Date of birth:                          Current age:
Presenting complaint:


Medical history:
Medication taken:
Family history:


Social history:


Date of session:
Details of treatment:

---

Figure 16. Sample case history sheet.

### Keeping client contact details

Whatever system you adopt for recording your client contact details, try to keep it as simple as possible. Aim to minimise the number of times you have to record the same details, for example by limiting the number of places in which you store your clients' contact details to no more than two places – such as stored on your phone and on your client's case history sheet. Keeping these details in a maximum of two places will cut down on any updating time and should mean that you will be less likely to forget to update *all* the contact records.

### Keeping client treatment records

If you always work from home then you will be able to keep all your client records together either in your filing cabinet, if you keep paper copies, or on your computer. However, if you work from two or more locations, work from your clients' homes or have a totally mobile practice, you will need to keep your client data in a way that you can easily carry it around with you. This could mean that you will find it more efficient to keep your client case history records on your laptop computer, and also store their contact details on your mobile phone so that you can make any quick calls whilst travelling or when working from different locations.

### What should I include in my client treatment records?

When you record your client sessions you should include an overview of your client treatment plan, and any particular techniques that you used, or supplements or herbs you may have prescribed. You may also find it helpful to document your clients' responses or outline their possible future needs or how their treatment could be developed. This will, of course, differ according to the therapy you are practising.

*Remember* – it's good practice to keep your notes as accurate and clearly written as possible, as your client records may be called in evidence in a court of law or for a professional conduct complaints hearing. It is therefore best to develop good habits early on.

### Client records – the golden rules

**The key points you should take note of are:**

♦ All your records should be factual and accurately record your session with your client – including the details of any treatments and responses. You should also include the date (and if appropriate, the time) of the session.

♦ Your records should be easily legible, either typed or handwritten in ink and not pencil – this is so that none of your notes can be erased.

♦ You should include full details of your client's treatment plan i.e. what issues did the client present with? What treatment did you give? What follow-up work do you intend? Document any decisions which were made and whether any information was shared with others.

♦ If you have had any contact with the client in between sessions, for example phone calls, emails or letters – make sure you write these up or include a copy of the correspondence and your response in the client's file.

♦ If you use abbreviations, you should make sure that these are consistent – and if you have your own form of abbreviating certain words or statements make sure you include a breakdown of what these are describing.

- Don't include any comments which are speculative rather than factual, or which could be taken to be offensive.

- Any mistakes in your handwritten notes should be crossed out – don't use Tippex to mask the mistake.

- Try to get into the good habit of allowing time at the end of each session to write up your notes as soon as the client has left.

- You should also keep copies of your diaries or appointment records. Make a note beside each entry as to whether the appointment was kept. If the appointment was cancelled, make a note of the reason for the cancellation.

> As a qualified therapist you have a legal and professional duty of care, and you need to ensure that your records reflect this. If anything err on the side of too much information rather than too little, for the general view that the courts take is that if something has not been recorded, it has not been done.

If you are still in any doubt as to the degree of detail you need to keep, you might like to raise this matter with your training school or tutor. *I usually work to the worst case scenario – if I had to present in court the details of my contact with a client, how useful and efficient are the details I have recorded?* I generally find that this helps to focus my mind appropriately – effectively preventing me from recording extraneous information, or recording anything that I wouldn't want the client to read or become public knowledge.

> Keep to the facts – remember your clients have a legal right to view their records.

### Keeping your client records safe and secure

If you keep a paper-based client record system, you should make sure that all documents are kept locked away in a metal filing cabinet when not in use. If your records are kept on computer, then you should ensure that access to all records is password protected, and that the records themselves are encrypted. You should also get into the habit of using a password protected screensaver so that if you have your computer running while you leave the room for a few moments when you have a client in the room, you can switch the screensaver on and protect your clients' files from being viewed or tampered with by any other person.

If you keep your records on computer you should get into a regular routine of 'good housekeeping' as soon as possible. This means:

- creating directory and file structures that are relevant to your work
- creating backups of all your files
- creating an archive for your client records which are no longer active
- clearing down your emails and filing any emailed client correspondence appropriately.

You should create a backup of all your files on at least a weekly basis, and keep the backups for the previous three weeks in case any of your data did not transfer correctly or has since become damaged or corrupted. You may find it more useful to keep client records which are no longer active within an 'archive' on your computer instead of relying on CDs or floppy disks for storage in order to save any problems in respect of physical storage, the potential for mistakenly overwriting files, the usual problems inherent in data transfer and, depending on how the CDs or floppies are stored, the potential for damaged or corrupted data.

### How long do I need to keep my client records?

This is a difficult question to answer with total authority as there is no legal requirement to keep your client records for a defined period of time. Insurance companies will advise that these records should be kept for as long as you possibly can because of the potential of a claim being made against you even if it is several years since you treated the claimant. Therefore you should keep these records for long as it is practicable for you to do so.

## Data Protection Act (DPA)

The Data Protection Act 1998 requires anyone who processes personal data to register with the Information Commissioner as a data controller unless they are exempt. Failure to notify is a criminal offence. Under the terms of this Act a *data controller* is taken to be anyone who decides the purposes for which any personal data is processed and the manner in which it is processed. And *personal data* is taken to mean any data which relates to a living individual who can be identified from that data and any other information which may be in the possession of the data controller.

The principles of data protection state that anyone processing personal data must ensure that the data is:

+ fairly and lawfully processed
+ processed for limited purposes
+ adequate, relevant and not excessive
+ accurate
+ not kept longer than necessary
+ processed in accordance with the data subject's rights
+ secure
+ not transferred to countries without adequate protection.

This Act gives clients the right to view their case history records. If a client wants to see their records, they must request this in writing. You will then have a maximum of 40 days in which to respond to this request. For further information about the DPA, see Chapter 12.

Most complementary therapists are not required to notify any manual records, however you can choose to notify them voluntarily. If you store your records or process your personal data on a computer, laptop or palmtop device, you will need to register. Registration currently costs £35 per year (no VAT), and you can register over the internet or by phone. The DPA website contains a handy on-line questionnaire which you can work through to assess whether or not you need to register.

## Financial records

> **You will need to keep records of all your income and expenditure from your business so that you can prove, if required to do so, the validity of your accounts.**

### Keeping records of your income and expenditure

Whatever methods you use for your financial record-keeping you will need to be able to prove your business income and expenditure. This means that even if your accounts are kept on computer, you will still need to keep physical copies of any receipts, bills, statements or invoices you have received.

You can set up systems for this quite simply. In order to prove your income you will need to be able to present a receipt or invoice for every payment you have received. This means issuing receipts to clients for each session and keeping a copy, and also keeping a copy of any invoices you have raised to companies or individuals in respect of your services. The simplest method of keeping track of your receipts is to use a duplicate book. You can then quickly issue a receipt for each payment you receive and automatically have a duplicate entry to tie in with your records.

You will then need a system for keeping all your receipts and bills etc. A simple system, and a good routine to get into is to put all your receipts, bills, invoices and statements into a box file, which you have set aside for this purpose, at the end of each working day. This will enable you to quickly sort through all the documents at the end of the week in order to enter these details into your accounts and file the documents accordingly. Make sure that you keep your box file locked away in your filing cabinet when you are not working on your documents. For further details about keeping accounts and using spreadsheets, see Chapter 5.

### How long do I need to keep these records?

You will need to keep copies of all your financial records for at least six years – this is the current year plus the five years prior to the latest date for returning your tax return – this a legal requirement.

## Training records

You will need to keep records of all your training, no matter what form this has taken, so that you can prove how much time you have spent being trained, or what activities you have been engaged in that will add credits towards your continued professional development (CPD). Each organisation you are a member of will have its own criteria for activities which count towards your CPD total and will also determine how many credits or hours you need to complete each year – you will need to comply with this in order to maintain your membership.

It's good practice to have copies of your professional qualifications on general display in your practice rooms so that your clients can check your details – select only those certificates for display which you feel are the most appropriate.

### *Keeping your training records*

All you need for keeping your training records is an A4 ring binder and some plastic pockets to keep your paperwork in. As most training courses will now provide you with a certificate of attendance, or if you have gone for a more in-depth training course a certificate detailing your new qualifications, it makes more sense to keep your training records in a paper-based system.

Depending on the amount of training you do in any one year, you might want to keep each year's training in a separate ring binder for ease of use. Keep a summary of your training for the year in the front of the binder. **You can keep this in a simple log format as detailed below (Figure 17).**

| |
|---|
| Name<br>Training log – Year |
| **Date**:<br>Title of training course, or details of activity:<br><br>Duration of course  Total hours:<br><br>Qualification gained: |
| **Date**:<br>Title of training course, or details of activity:<br><br>Duration of course  Total hours:<br><br>Qualification gained: |
| **Date**:<br>Title of training course, or details of activity:<br><br>Duration of course  Total hours:<br><br>Qualification gained: |
| Total credits for year = |

Figure 17. Training log.

*You may find it helpful to include a note of the minimum number of credits, or hours spent in training, that you will need to have completed in order to comply with membership requirements.*

### How long do I need to keep these records?

It's a good idea to keep these records for the entirety of your career as a complementary therapist. Whenever you change your professional membership from one organisation to another, you will need to be able to confirm all the dates of the training you have undertaken, the subjects or areas you have trained in and also be able to produce any certificates or qualifications that you may have received.

## Insurance records

You will need to keep records of any contact you have had with your insurance company or brokers, as well as details of any insurance claims you may have made or may have been made against you along with copies of all your policies, certificates and any endorsements.

> **Your current professional insurance certificates and endorsements to your policies should be on general display in your practice room, so that any clients can check you are appropriately insured.**

### Keeping your insurance records

It is often easier to keep these records in a paper-based system, otherwise you are likely to end up with a mixture of paper and computer files. You might find it helpful to keep all your insurance correspondence and certificates for each financial year together in one ring binder. Copies of your policies and any endorsement details will usually remain in force unless they have been amended in some way (in which case you will be sent new copies), and therefore should continue to be filed with your current year's documents until any such changes are made. Any details relating to claims made by clients might be more appropriately filed in with your client's case history records. All your insurance records should be kept in a locked filing cabinet.

### How long do I need to keep these records?

There is no legal requirement to keep these documents for a specified period of time, however it is good practice to keep these records for as long as you possibly can in case a claim is made against you.

## Professional membership records and certificates

You will need to keep details of any professional memberships you hold, copies of any correspondence you have had regarding your membership and any certificates confirming your membership and the designations you are permitted to use after your name.

It's good practice to have your professional membership certificates on general display in your office, as your clients can then view the professional organisations you belong to and the level of your current membership.

### Keeping your membership records

It is generally simpler to keep all these records together in a paper-based system. As you are unlikely to have much in the way of any correspondence to keep, and your membership certificates are usually current for as long as you are a fully paid-up member of that organisation, you may find that if you review all your documents on a regular basis you can keep everything in just one file.

### How long do I need to keep these records?

You will need to keep these records for at least as long as you are a member of a particular organisation. You may find it helpful to keep these records for the entirety of your career, for example, for biographical or CV purposes.

## Keeping, storing and disposing of records

### Keeping your records

The length of time that you need to keep your records for will vary according to the type of record and whether there is a legal requirement to store certain records for a particular length of time. **Unless you have been advised by a professional on the length of time to keep a particular set of records, the usual requirements are:**

- **client records:** no legally determined storage time – keep indefinitely, or for as long as is practicable

- **financial records:** legal requirement to keep records of your accounts for at least five years prior to the latest date for returning your tax return
- **training records:** no legally determined storage time – keep for duration of your career
- **insurance records:** no legally determined storage time – keep indefinitely, or for as long as is practicable
- **membership records:** no legally determined storage time – keep for duration of your career.

## Storing your records safely

> All your records need to be kept safely in order to ensure client confidentiality and also to prevent any interruption to your business through the loss of any data.

Paper records should always be kept locked away in a metal filing cabinet when not in use, as should any floppy disks or CDs. Any computer-based records should be password protected and computer files should be encrypted. You should take regular backups of all your computer files, at the very least on a weekly basis. And if your computer system is the main store for your records and the means by which you process all your data, you should also ensure that you keep a copy of the registration details for any software that you have bought and the registration keys for any shareware that you have purchased. For more information about encryption software, see Chapter 12.

## Disposing of your records safely

You should ensure that you dispose of your records in a safe and secure way. **For security reasons your:**

- paper records should be shredded
- CDs should be shredded or snapped in half
- floppy disks or hard drives should have a low-level erasure applied to them (for further information on how to do this, consult the manual for your operating system).

> If you sell your computer and haven't cleared the hard drive down appropriately, the new user will be able to access your old files even if you deleted them before you passed the equipment over.

# CHAPTER SEVEN

# Training and Professional Development

## Why do I need further training?

As a professional, you need to keep up with the latest developments in your chosen field. Clients are generally very well read, and will often present you with quite challenging comments and questions, so you need to be prepared.

However well qualified you are when you start your practice you should still give some thought to your future development. Many professional organisations insist that their members spend a specified minimum amount of time each year in continued personal development (CPD) in order to comply with membership requirements. However, despite any formal need for further training or qualifications, if you genuinely want to 'grow' both your practice and yourself, you should be seeking out fresh challenges on a regular basis. These can either be some formal training, or can be new experiences such as running workshops or writing a book. The more experienced you are, the more techniques you have at your disposal for helping your clients reach their full potential and overcome their problems. Experience aids creativity, and the more creative you become, the more individual and personal is your approach to your work.

## What kind of training should I invest in?

**Further training can take many forms:**

- further professional training in your particular therapy
- training in associated therapies
- experiential training
- researching and writing

- teaching and mentoring
- supervision and peer group support
- egroups and newsletters
- keeping self-development and training logs.

### Further professional training

You may already be quite clear as to your immediate training requirements, but may not have considered your future needs or the strategic path you wish to take. If you need to do some further work on this, see Chapter 10 for some ideas to help you formulate your plans. If you have decided on a particular specialism, or are aware of the next step on your career path, it will be easier to decide on the appropriate courses to help you achieve your aims.

### Where can I find a training course?

Many of the schools or organisations that you trained with will have other courses, workshops or seminars offering you a chance to develop your skills further. For example, a hypnotherapist might want to specialise in rebirthing or past life regression, a healer might want to extend their work by healing animals, an aromatherapist might want a course to help them work more effectively with clients with learning disabilities.

Various training courses are listed on internet complementary health directories, for example, Healthy Pages and Positive Health (see Chapter 12 for the website addresses). You could also check out the various complementary health, and professional therapy, journals. Friends or colleagues may be able to recommend relevant courses to you, and will be able to advise you on which ones they found the most useful. If you are a member of any therapy-based egroups, you could ask the group for advice and recommendations.

### Checking the course before you book

It is always a good idea to check various details about the course before you confirm your booking to make sure that you are getting good value for your money. Whatever course or further training you decide on make sure it is properly accredited, and check the qualifications of the trainers to ensure that your training will be conducted at an appropriate level. *Be clear about what you want to gain from the course before you book it.* If the course prospectus does not cover all your points, raise any questions with the trainers.

### Training in associated therapies

If you undertake further training in therapies associated with your main practice work, this will obviously increase your portfolio of skills and the range of therapies you can offer. In addition you will often find that you can mix and match techniques from one therapy to another if you take a creative approach. For example, a massage therapist might also decide to train in Bach flower remedies or aromatherapy. These skills can then be brought creatively into the massage session by recommending Bach flower remedies which might help your client to deal with their negative thought patterns, or using aromatherapy oils as a 'background' scent to increase the relaxing effect of the massage or to help clear a client's blocked sinuses.

### The benefits of practising more than one therapy

By blending therapies in this way you are helping your sessions to become more effective, and you're adding value to the sessions for your clients. The other benefits to this approach are that you will often gain an increase in clients (and thereby income) due to the unique way in which you work. If your clients enjoy the way you blend therapies to suit their individual needs, they are more likely to recommend you to others. And if you develop this approach further, there is the potential for you to teach your specialised techniques, or particular ways of working, to other therapists in your field. You could also develop training manuals or write some articles, or even a book, on the subject.

> If you have trained in an additional related therapy then you may get clients coming to you for that therapy alone, so you have automatically boosted your client base.

Do make sure that any further therapies you add to your skills base complement your main therapy practice. There is little to be gained from training in a number of unrelated therapies, as some clients may regard this unfavourably and believe that you have less expertise than someone specialising in one or two related therapies.

### Experiential training

This is so often overlooked that I believe it deserves a special mention. Too often we focus on a particular course of training for the known skills or qualifications that completing the course will give us. Whilst this is all well and good, it fulfils a very narrow interpretation of what *training* can be. Experiential training is training on the job, a somewhat old-fashioned concept in this era but still a very effective way of learning.

### Why should I seek out this kind of training?

There will be many occasions in the course of your development when this can be a very useful way in which to boost your skills. For the newly-qualified practitioner, it allows a 'honeymoon' period during which they can have the reassuring benefit of a much more experienced therapist close to hand, or on call, to help with any problems or to clarify any techniques or processes. For more experienced practitioners it can allow you the chance to study someone else's techniques first hand and to assimilate the best, or the most relevant aspects of their style or method of working, into your own practice. In this situation you are more or less 'apprenticing' yourself to the other practitioner.

This means of developing your skills need not cost a lot. Some practitioners will not charge anything for this kind of learning experience, whereas others will allow you to barter, for example you help out with some of their basic administration work for an agreed block of time, or you act as an unpaid assistant on any workshops or training courses that they are running.

*You can also self-train by using this method.* For example, you might have put together some new techniques which you would like to test for their effectiveness. In order to gain some experience with these techniques, you could offer free sessions to clients who have the particular problem or medical condition that you want to treat. Try advertising locally for people who are willing to volunteer to try out your new processes. This will help you to manage any client expectations about the treatment and will give you a proper chance to assess the effectiveness of your techniques.

### What other use can I make of this kind of training?

You could also try out any ideas for a new workshop by running a shortened version of the course, free to anyone who would like to learn those new skills, or you could decide to run the full version on a donation only basis. This way you get to run your workshop for real, so your training needs are met, you also get to learn of any potential problems with the course as well as the things which went well so you can make any necessary adjustments or amendments before you run the course as a paying concern. Your course participants also benefit, as they get to learn some new skills, such as basic relaxation techniques, either for free or for the price of a small donation.

**The more obvious spin-offs of this kind of training are:** teaching your 'new' techniques to other therapists, and writing books or articles on your work and findings. And for those of you with a suitable statistics and research background, this can lead to the publication of scientific-based research in related therapeutic and medical journals, which will help you to further develop your practice. The complementary therapy world tends to suffer from a lack of scientific rigour in the documenting and researching of the efficacy of various techniques and practices, so any detailed statistical studies are very welcome.

### Researching and writing

This is an excellent way in which you can boost your CPD rating, gain further income, increase your practice, add on a specialism and generally widen your skills base. And the even better news is that you can often fit this around your working day by using any gaps or missed appointments as brilliant opportunities for furthering your research.

### Writing articles

You can start out in a small way by writing the occasional articles for therapy or health journals. You will need to have something new to say, or a new slant on a set of techniques, or be able to detail the processes you utilise for certain medical conditions. You will also need to make sure that your article is supported with appropriate research findings and data.

You can also try writing articles for local newspapers or community magazines. If you are lucky you may be offered a regular weekly or monthly slot, writing on various medical complaints or common problems and how these can be treated by various complementary therapies. You must be prepared to research outside of your chosen field of study in order to present a well-balanced article with maximum appeal.

*Any articles you write can also be posted up on your website.* If your website does not already include articles on the various conditions you commonly work with in your practice, now's the time to start thinking about including a section for this. This will not only boost the value of your website to any interested potential clients, it will also prove your on-going interest in your clients' problems and health issues. Include links to other sites where relevant. If you include a section on your website specifically for other therapists, you can use some of your articles to stimulate debate and an information flow on a particular topic you are researching – again another very simple way of increasing your learning curve.

### *Writing manuals*

Once you've tried a few articles, you may also like to consider writing a training manual – perhaps outlining a particular process you use, or detailing how to run a workshop on a particular issue. These do not have to be great heavy tomes, instead go for a maximum of approximately 30 pages. This will then allow you to run off paper copies fairly easily to post to purchasers, or to produce the training as an ebook. For more details about producing ebooks, see Chapter 12.

### *Writing books*

There is also the option of producing your own book on a health or therapy related topic. If this seems a daunting idea you might want to consider the possibility of sharing the work with another therapist. This in itself is a unique learning experience, for if you are writing with another more experienced therapist you have the potential for learning a lot more. In general, any research and writing you do is unlikely to gain you a lot of money, but you will be experience-rich and furthering your development. For further information about writing a book, see Chapter 12.

### *Teaching and mentoring*

Once you feel you've reached a suitable level of experience you may want to consider teaching or mentoring other students and therapists. As well as being another source of income, this will cause you to revisit your knowledge base to update and expand it, thereby enhancing your own development.

**Teaching**

Teaching will require you to hone your presentation and analytical skills, and if you feel you are somewhat lacking in this department you might find it helpful to take a course in presentation skills or to run your first few teaching seminars or workshops with another more experienced colleague. Keep a self-development journal, and make sure you note down after each workshop or seminar those areas you need to develop further – whether this is your research or knowledge base, or more practical skills. Don't forget to also note down any learning points, for example, how you dealt with a particularly difficult individual, or how getting the group to reflect on what they had learnt just before lunch sent everyone off in a more positive mood. *This way everything you do becomes a creative tool for your own growth and development.*

## Mentoring

Mentoring or supervising therapy students is an excellent way of adding to your portfolio of skills. If you feel you have the appropriate experience, make an approach to the schools or organisations you trained with, or any other bodies you are a member of or are affiliated to. Do note that you will need to satisfy their criteria for supervisors, and this may involve you taking an appropriate training course.

If your own organisation, or previous training school, doesn't already have a supervision scheme, here's an opportunity to set one up for them. Mentoring, or supervision, is challenging work, and it will cause you to further your research and push your personal boundaries. Your student will benefit from the experience and so will you. I've found the questions students have raised during supervision sessions have prompted me to devise workshops on related topics, to compile basic training manuals on various techniques, and have also prompted articles and books.

## *Personal supervision and peer group meetings*

This is another way in which you can develop your skills, explore new processes and get some personalised training.

## Personal supervision

Undergoing personal supervision, whether it is conducted one-to-one or in a group, is a chance for you to offload some of the problems you may have encountered in your work, to seek further advice on how to progress issues, and it also provides you with a forum for any subjects you wish to raise. The amount of supervision you will need to undergo on a regular basis will depend on the therapy you work in and the membership requirements of any organisations you belong to.

One-to-one sessions will give you a chance to seek further information from your supervisor. For example, they may recommend books or articles which could give you greater insight into how to handle particular situations, or more in-depth knowledge of certain medical conditions that you have encountered in your work. Your supervisor may also be willing to share some of their on-going research with you, or even ask you to help out with workshops they may be running. Your supervisor may also offer you the chance of some personalised training in new techniques or processes. *Supervision sessions can be a goldmine for new ideas and will help to shape your thinking on difficult issues – so use your time to the full.* Don't be afraid to 'shop around' for a supervisor who best fits your needs, or even swap between two or three supervisors according to their skills and your requirements.

**Peer group meetings**

Even if your particular area of work does not require that you undergo regular supervision, you might find it helpful to explore the idea of meeting up with fellow practitioners on a regular basis – effectively setting up a peer group. If you set a clear agenda for your meetings you can get every participant to bring something of value with them to the meeting, for example, a summary of a book they have just read that they want to recommend to the group, or a new process they have developed which can be demonstrated to the group.

With everyone's agreement these meetings could sometimes be turned into mini-workshops on themed topics. At other times the meetings could be used as a brain-storming exercise for exploring better ways of dealing with some client issues, or they could be a chance to learn from others about new marketing tips. To keep the group dynamic, look for different themes each time you meet, agree to meet on a regular basis and alternate where you meet between all the members so that no one is constantly hosting these sessions. *The beauty of this arrangement is the flexibility it offers and the enormous potential for personal development and training – but it only works well if all members contribute to each session.*

Group meetings or peer supervision are a low cost training option. If you keep the numbers small, for example no more than ten, you can arrange to meet in each others' houses thereby cutting the cost or the need to hire a meeting room specially. The only other costs will be the costs to the individual for producing whatever it is that they want to share with the group – such as: printing out details of any process they want to showcase, producing small samples of blended oils, or creating any CDs and tapes that they wish to share.

### Egroups and newsletters

The free flow of information within an egroup, and the informative articles, tips and hints that newsletters often contain, can provide you with another low-cost way of furthering your development.

**Egroups**

If you're not already a member of an egroup for your therapy, now is the time to join an existing group or maybe set one up yourself. If you are thinking of setting one up yourself you will need to set some basic rules, for example, determining what sort of issues can be discussed by the group, what kind of material can be shared, and what support or help members of the group can expect to receive or give. If the school or organisation you trained with doesn't already have its own egroup, you might want to suggest setting one up for them. This will have the added benefit of allowing you access to a database of potential members who may wish to join the group. For more information about setting up egroups, see Chapter 12.

*These groups will offer advice and support other members who may be experiencing problems in their work.* For example, a more experienced member of the group may email a brief response to a request for help on a particular problem, another member of the group may publish some useful links to other sites or training courses, someone else may use the group in order to showcase their latest research and request other members critique their findings.

## Newsletters

A group of local therapists could think about producing their own newsletter, which could include a FAQs (frequently asked questions) sheet on a particular topic or a list of that month's top ten tips. This could then be circulated to all the members of the group for their information and be used as a way to add to existing skills. This can work in a similar way to the group meeting – but this time *a different person is tasked each month to take responsibility for compiling the newsletter and to seek out some newsworthy ideas from other members of the group.*

### *Self-development and training log*

Whatever training or development exercises you undertake, it will help your overall future growth if you keep a self-development and training log. This is simply a record of 'learning' points you have become aware of during any training or supervision. For example, after reviewing a demonstration of some new techniques that you gave to students you realise that the demonstration could have been better had you planned certain aspects of it more fully, and you can also remember how feeling nervous throughout the whole demonstration meant you didn't give of your best. Your learning points from that demonstration might be to allocate more time for planning and to review how you could present certain areas of your demonstration more effectively. You might also include a note of your need for some confidence boosting or training in presentation skills in order to help overcome the 'stage fright'. These insights regarding your possible future development and training needs should be entered in your log so that you can then take these further.

Your entries don't always have to point out a training need. Sometimes you will want to note down an action you made, or an example you gave on the spur of the moment which had a good result. **Note these down as well, as in Figure 18 below, as they will then remind you to incorporate these actions and examples into the mainstream of your work.**

---

Sample – personal development and training log

Date: 29 February 2003

Activity: Demonstrating 'colour' breathing techniques.

Learning points: Need for better preparation – students asked if there were any pre-printed notes on the techniques that they could take away and study.

Action to take: Carefully consider before next demonstration or workshop what prep work I can do to help the learning process for the students.

Action taken: I've written a set of notes to accompany the next 'colour' breathing techs demo – now need to bring this action forward into my training plans so that I plan and allocate time to complete the notes for the other demos and workshops.

---

Figure 18. Sample log.

It's good practice to review your training log on a regular basis, in order that any immediate problems can be addressed. Any sizeable chunks of training you require, or costly courses, should be incorporated into your annual business and financial plans.

## How should I plan my training?

Whether you decide to book a particular training course or to use some more informal methods of self development, make sure you maximise what you will be getting for your money or time by doing a little bit of planning first.

### Planning for regular training

It's often best to do your training planning at the beginning of the year, whether you take this to be January or the beginning of your financial year. Have some key subjects in mind (you might want to check your training log for any particular requirements) and then assess what is on offer. For example, is there a particular specialism that you would like to develop? If you tie this in with your overall business plans you will be clearer about how much you can afford to spend on your training and personal development. You will also need to take into account how you are going to meet the CPD requirements of any organisations you belong to. Remember, this can be achieved in a number of ways which do not necessarily require you to spend money on attending a training course. Professionally, you may have been set a minimum amount of training that you need to comply with, but on a personal level you may decide that you want to improve on those figures by some creative training of your own.

## Make provision for your training

First of all ensure that you have made provision in your training plan to meet any minimum requirements and are clear about which courses, or action, this will require you taking and when. Make sure you put these dates in your diary or year planner so that they are kept free and also so that you can then see what space you have left to fit in those other training or experience needs. A good rule of thumb is to allow 10% of your work time for training and continuing your professional development – effectively 'tithing' time for personal and professional growth. *There are many ways in which you can creatively use this time*, and you might find you make better use of your time if you block out one half day each week for this purpose as this will allow you to maintain your focus.

## Set your training plan for the year

This could be as simple as prioritising five key areas or topics which you want to research further, develop your skills around or seek formal training in. How you mix and match this is up to you, but make sure that you include a variety of ways in which you will achieve your priorities, for example:

- **practical skills** – trying out new techniques on volunteers
- **researching** – on a particular medical condition
- **formal training courses** – such as counselling or life-coaching
- **experiencing** – running a workshop for the first time with a more experienced colleague
- **writing** – a manual about your new techniques.

## Don't overstretch yourself

Make sure you are not overstretching yourself with the priorities you have set. If you are in any doubt about this, determine the top three topics that you really want to achieve and allow yourself to put the rest on hold knowing that you can go back to these should time permit. If you have allocated a regular half day slot each week for training, it is now a simple matter to go back to your diary or year planner and pencil in these topics. You might also like to consider how much time you allocate for the completion of each topic. Any dates or timescales that you pencil in should act as guides only – allow them to be flexible benchmarks for achieving your training priorities.

### What training would benefit me the most?

Whatever future training courses you may choose, be very clear before booking about what you wish to gain from the course. Ask yourself how it will aid you in your work. How will you be able to integrate this new knowledge into your sessions? If you're not clear about any of these points, give the course organisers a call and get them to explain the course more fully and put those questions to them – if they're not clear about the purpose and benefits of the course you might be well advised to look for a similar course elsewhere.

Apply the same logical analysis to training which does not take the form of a formal training course. Your time is precious, so ensure that whatever form of training you are engaged in it meets your strategic goals

### Affording the training

Training and personal development and growth are very important, not just in business terms but also for you to both expand and balance the way in which you work, and the way in which you operate as an individual. Therefore, do make sure that you reflect this importance in the amount of money you are prepared to spend. Use that 10% rule again, and allow 10% of your income to go towards future development each year. Initially it might seem a lot, but this basic 'tithing' rule has worked well for me and for others. Of course, if you are unable to afford the full 10% in any one year than you always have the option of seeking out those cheaper ways of achieving further development.

If some courses you would like to do are too expensive to undertake in any one particular year, you will need to decide whether that training goes on your 'wish' list; whether there is an equally good course which is financially more affordable, or whether there is a short 'taster' or foundation course in the same subject which might fill some gaps in your knowledge base until such time as you can afford the main course. You might also be able to do some 'on the job training' with an experienced practitioner in that field for minimal cost.

If you decide however that despite the high cost, *that* training course is an absolute must as it will repay itself several times over in the first year after training, give some thought to taking out a loan to cover the cost. If you have done your research correctly about the potential benefits of the course you will be in a good position to persuade your bank manager to loan you the money.

# CHAPTER EIGHT

# Good Business Practice

## First impressions count

How you run your practice will have a considerable impact on how profitable it becomes, as first impressions are so important. This includes basics such as how you greet your clients on the phone and in person, how professional your business stationery is, whether you run your sessions to time, as well as higher level aspects such as ensuring your clients' confidentiality and keeping your personal training up to date. Even the name you give to your business will have an impact on its future development.

**The following are some of the key areas you may wish to review in order to assess how well these enhance or detract from the image you wish to portray:**

- the name of your practice
- the working environment
- how you run your sessions
- how you handle bookings
- your business stationery
- how easy it is for your clients to get in contact with you
- how you run your practice.

## Naming your business

It is very important that you consider carefully how you are going to name your business, for you need to ensure that the name will convey all the right messages and present a positive image. It is always a good feature to include wording in the title which gives some idea of what your business is about, for example, a hypnotherapist might use the word *trance*, *hypno* or *hypnotherapy* in the business name, other practitioners might use the words *alternative* or *complementary*, or include a pairing of the locality with their particular therapy, for example, Anytown Acupuncture Centre.

Once you have chosen a name you must be prepared to stick with it – changing the name at a later date can prove to be expensive, both in terms of money as well as your business reputation.

You need to make sure that no one else in the same line of business is using that name already, so check the local telephone and trade directories, and also check on the internet. If you are thinking of advertising or marketing any of your products on the internet, once you've chosen your business name purchase a personalised domain name for your business which relates to this.

## The working environment

One of the keys to running a successful practice is comfort – if you look after your clients' needs you will automatically be viewed as caring and empathic.

Whether you are working from home, within a clinic or have your own set of offices, it is essential that you provide the correct environment for your clients. Your practice room must always be clean and tidy. And while decoration is very much an individual choice, you should consider that not all your clients may share your taste in colours or design. Light, neutral colours are always a safe bet. *Avoid visual 'clutter'* – a small number of appropriate pictures, paintings or certificates on your walls is fine, but be selective or this can become overwhelming.

### *Furniture and equipment*

The furniture and equipment in your room should be functional, comfortable and clean. If you use a couch for massage or healing, make sure you have a set of steps to help your clients get on and off the couch safely. Keep a variety of chairs in your room – some of your clients may find it hard to get out of a low armchair, others may find chairs without arms more practical. Switch off any unnecessary electrical equipment while you are working with a client in order to prevent any unnecessary background noise and to create a more peaceful environment whilst you work. If you use a lot of electrical equipment you may also want to consider investing in an ioniser to reduce the static charge in your room.

### Making the room more comfortable

Your working area should be adequately lit, and appropriately heated. You might want to add other touches, such as using plug-in air fresheners, or burning essential oils. These can be helpful for setting a calm, relaxed mood, and they can also act as positive triggers – clients will frequently link a particularly pleasing smell or a piece of music (if you use music in your work) to being in a relaxed state and will often mention how good it makes them feel. Plants can help to energise a room, create a splash of colour and some can also be good for reducing the less than desirable effects of all your electrical equipment (think computers – think spider plants). But do be aware that some of your clients may have allergies to flowering plants so you might want to consider an artificial arrangement instead.

### Using music

Using music in your sessions can help to relax a client and set a calm and peaceful mood for your sessions. *Choose your music with care.* Instrumental pieces are usually a better choice than sung pieces, as the words of a song may not be conveying the right message or may prove to be a distraction.

If you are going to use music in your sessions or as background noise in your waiting area, you should be aware that this constitutes a 'public performance' and you should therefore register with the Performing Right Society and pay the appropriate annual licence fee – this is not very expensive. Alternatively, you can download music from the internet, or buy CDs and tapes of music which is royalty free – you pay a one-off payment and can use the music in whatever way you choose. For details of the Performing Right Society and royalty free music, see Chapter 12.

### Subconscious messages

You should also consider what subconscious messages you may be sending out by the personal touches you add to your room. If you have photos of your family on open display, these may send unintentional signals to clients who are single, newly bereaved or who have relationship problems – triggering emotions or sending signals counter to your equality policy, so choose carefully. The same goes for pictures or posters which may have symbolic meanings.

### Free from noise

Your practice room should be as free from noisy distractions as possible. If you have a waiting room, check whether any conversations can be overheard in your practice room. *If you can hear other people's conversations through the walls, the chances are that they can hear yours.* You need to ensure that any information your client shares with you is treated confidentially, so you may need to consider relocating the waiting room or playing some light music to mask being overheard.

Your working area also needs to be as accessible as possible (see Chapter 1 for details about access for people with disabilities), preferably located on the ground floor or with adequate access for wheelchair users. Ensure that the toilets are nearby, that there are facilities for disabled users and that you have somewhere to wash your hands. If you don't have a designated kitchen area you might find it useful to set aside some space in your room for making hot drinks.

## Your session charges

Make sure you set clear guidelines regarding your sessions. List your fees, any cancellation policies you might have, how long your sessions last, the hours you work, how you work, whether you offer an initial free consultation and detail what the client can expect from a session. If you offer more than one therapy you will need to make these details clear for each therapy.

### Fees

Investigate how much, and how, other local practitioners charge and then charge for your work accordingly. **Other decisions you will need to make are whether to:**

◆ offer a free initial consultation
◆ charge more for evening and weekend sessions
◆ offer any discounts
◆ charge for cancelled or missed appointments.

### Receipts and appointment cards

Once your client has paid for the session make sure you provide them with a receipt. **This can also include messages and reminders, such as:**

◆  details of your cancellation policy

◆  a reminder of the date and time for the next appointment

◆  a reminder of any 'homework' that your client has been asked to do.

If your receipts are business card size and printed on card, they are less likely to get lost or mislaid by the client as the card will fit neatly into a purse or wallet.

### Free initial consultation

Offering a free initial consultation is often a good selling point. In practical terms it will also give you a chance to explore your client's problems before deciding to take them on and allow your client the chance to meet you in person. It also gives you the opportunity to discuss how your therapy could potentially help the client with their issues. It's good practice to leave some extra time after the initial consultation in case the client would like to go straight ahead with a session, as they may have travelled quite a distance to get to you.

### Discounts

You may decide to offer discounts to clients who book and pay for a block of sessions, or people on low incomes such as pensioners, students and those on benefits. If you decide to offer discounts you will also need to decide how many sessions in a week, or month, you can afford to discount in this way. If the number of discounted sessions exceeds that which is sustainable, operate a waiting list and get back in touch with those potential clients when the numbers have balanced out again.

### Cancellation policy

There are always going to be situations in life which will cause your clients to cancel their appointments, so it's best to work out your cancellation policy ahead of time. Most therapists will not charge for cancellations providing the client has given 24 hours' notice. You may also decide to waive any charges if the cancellation is due to illness or if there's been a family emergency of some sort. Decide whether you are going to charge a nominal cancellation fee, the full fee, or a percentage of the full fee, and make your clients aware of your cancellation policy when they book a session.

### *Reminders*

Rather than deal with a cancellation, you may prefer to remind your client of their session in advance, by phoning them, or sending a text message or email. Although it is annoying to have to take responsibility from the client for this, at the end of the day you need to earn a living, so if you are going through a spell of clients missing sessions you might want to try this out. The same applies to clients who reschedule or book appointments over the phone. If you send out a postcard detailing their session date and time you are less likely to have them miss the next session.

## Your working week

Whilst a number of therapists work in a very flexible way, others prefer to work to a set pattern. Routine can be very helpful especially if you have a family to look after. It can also work in the favour of clients who want to have their 'slot' on a particular day and time each week. *Having a set working pattern may make it easier for you to set your boundaries, as it will help you to focus on completing your work during your work hours.* You will also need to decide what, if any, out of hours work you are prepared to offer for those clients who can't manage the usual daytime appointments.

Make sure you list your days and hours of work on your practice brochure and website. And if you are working at more than one location, list your venues and the relevant days and times you work at each.

### *Number and spacing of client sessions*

If you are working in a therapy which requires a number of sessions before any improvement is likely to be made, discuss these details at the initial consultation and make sure that they feature on your literature. Similarly if there is an average number of sessions that clients come to you for help with a particular problem, state this. It will make your job easier as this information will help to shape your clients' expectations of the therapy you offer.

#### Assessing number of sessions

When you first meet with a client it is always good practice to assess how many sessions the client is likely to need. Generalisations are acceptable, for example, telling the clients that for most presenting issues it's four to six sessions, but do state whether it is the case that some problems can be dealt with quicker and detail which problems might take longer – such as deep-seated psychological trauma or chronic medical conditions. This way clients can determine in advance whether they can afford a full course of sessions and you can discuss any discounts if applicable.

**Keeping a space between sessions**

The spacing between sessions is also important. Some therapies require a client to attend a session on a weekly basis, others which are looking for behavioural changes on the part of the client may require a minimum gap between sessions of two weeks in order to adequately assess the change process. The spacing between sessions is also important to a client from a financial point of view. If it isn't necessary for a client to attend once a week, let them know what is necessary rather than desirable as this may financially be in your best interests as well. A client may decide to go ahead with a course of treatment if they know the sessions can be spaced out to once a fortnight or even once a month.

*Keeping your sessions to time*

*Decide the duration of your sessions and stick to it.* For many therapies, working on an hourly basis works best – particularly if your therapy is quite exhausting or requires the client to concentrate for any length of time. Some therapies, such as massage therapy, will have differing times for sessions related to particular routines for different types of massage.

**Time-keeping**

Time-keeping during sessions is important. You need to be able to allocate some time within each of your sessions for discussing progress or any problems that your client may have been experiencing, and still leave sufficient time for the therapeutic work. Clients will have an increased respect for you as a professional if they are clear from the outset what to expect. Many clients may be trying to fit in sessions around work and home commitments; if you run your sessions over the allotted time you may be causing problems for your client rather than giving them added value.

**Allowing time for breaks**

Allow some time either side of each session in order that you can take a quick break, have a drink, make a quick phone call, go to the toilet etc before the next client arrives. Having this gap will also help smooth the situation when clients arrive late for sessions. Don't, however, feel duty bound to go through a complete session with a client who has arrived late – especially if this means you miss out on breaks or may need to keep your next client waiting. If you keep to time your clients will understand that the same is expected of them or otherwise they lose out. There will, of course, be occasions when you do decide to work extra time for a particular client, and that's fine – all part of the flexibility of the job – but just remember that you are running a business.

### Allowing time for the client's needs

If the nature of your work is such that your clients are likely to abreact, you may want to allow an extra ten to 15 minutes on each session to ensure that you have time to deal with this in a professional manner. Not only is it more professional to spend time settling the client before they leave, but it also helps build trust and will generally have the client talking about you and your practice in a positive way.

### Keeping accurate time

Many therapists find it useful to locate their clock on the wall just above where their client will be sitting – this way you can easily flick your glance from your client to the clock without obviously clock-gazing. If you need to move around whilst you work buy one of those watches of the sort which nurses use, attach it to your shirt or t-shirt and a quick glance will keep you updated.

If keeping to time is a difficult for you to achieve, you might want to think of using a watch, clock or timer with an inbuilt alarm which you can set to go off at predetermined intervals, for example, five to ten minutes before the end of every session. Make sure the alarm is not loud or intrusive in any way – though for those clients who like to chat you may find yourself grateful that they can hear an alarm as it can be a good prompt for them to move on. If noise is a potential issue, try to get a timer where the alarm vibrates rather than sounds.

## Handling bookings

Whether potential clients contact you by phone, email, in person or in writing, you need to have all the necessary details at your fingertips in order to present yourself in a professional fashion.

**Before you receive that first phone call or potential booking make sure you have:**

◆ decided on your charges and any discounts

◆ decided whether you are going to offer a free initial consultation

◆ the full postal address of your practice room

◆ details of how clients can get to you by public transport

◆ details of the nearest car parks if clients can't park outside your practice

◆ decided the hours which you are going to work

◆ formulated a short description of how you work and what your therapy entails.

> Clients are very quick to pick up on any vague statements, so don't allow any hesitation to creep into your voice, and make sure you know the answers to the above points off by heart.

### Putting together an initial booking package

Some clients may request further details about your therapy before deciding on whether to book a session, so it's a good idea to have a small package of information that you can quickly hand out or mail out.

**What should this include?**

◆ administrative details

◆ details about yourself as a therapist

◆ details about how you work

◆ details about specific problems or illnesses you treat

◆ your code of conduct

◆ any 'freebies'.

**Administrative details**

Administrative details include your costs, your contact details and full postal address of your practice, your cancellation policy, details of your NHS provider number and/or BUPA registration number if applicable, a map of your location, your hours of work, details of how to get to your practice by bus, train, car or tube.

**You the therapist**

Include a few paragraphs about how you work, whether you specialise in treating any particular problems or medical complaints, whether you combine therapies and if so which ones and how, how long you have been practising, where you trained, your qualifications and membership of any professional organisations, and include confirmation that you are insured.

### How you work

Confirm how long your sessions are, what techniques you are likely to use, what the client can expect during the session and whether the client should prepare themselves before the session in any way, for example, not eating for an hour before the session.

### Specific problems or illnesses

This could be a separate sheet giving a brief background to the problem, the current thinking on that issue, the possible remedies, how your therapy in particular could help the client and what successes you have had in the past – you could include any anecdotal evidence of change, specific statistics or any testimonials you may have received from clients. Include books or articles for further reading, and list relevant websites which may be able to offer further self-help.

### Code of conduct

This is a statement of your professional standards. It should include your confidentiality policy, your equalities policy and detail full information about how your practice is run and what your client can expect. For more information on codes of conduct, see Chapter 4.

### What's free?

You could include a pen (overprinted with your practice details), or an introductory discount voucher.

## Business stationery

A good layout and design for your business stationery is essential. Clever use of the same typeface, colours and logo on your stationery creates a positive professional image.

### Stationery – five golden rules

- make sure all your contact details are clearly displayed and easily legible
- decide on a style and layout and keep to it
- make sure your letterheads, compliment slips and envelopes match in colour and quality
- don't recycle old letterheads or envelopes
- keep an adequate supply in stock.

### Are your contact details clearly displayed?

Make sure that all your contact details are clearly displayed and easily legible on all your business stationery. This will help to distinguish your practice from that of any other therapist – as a client may have requested, or been given documents or leaflets from a number of sources.

> Remember your name or company title is part of your branding, so make sure it stands out – and include it on everything.

Keep on top of any changes to your details, whether these are changes to your practice address, telephone number or additional qualifications (if you list these).

### Layout and style

Layout and style help to define your image. Try out different styles and layouts until you decide on the one you would like to keep, and keep in mind the requirements of the Disability Discrimination Act. This Act places a requirement on all service providers to provide information in as accessible a manner as possible. This means you should:

- select sans serif fonts such as Arial or Verdana
- refrain from using underlining, italicised or capital letters
- choose good contrasting background and font colours
- ensure your general correspondence is written in font size 12 or larger.

These measures will help anyone who is visually impaired to access your information and services. For more information on the requirements of the Disability Discrimination Act, see Chapter 12.

**Do your letterheads and envelopes match?**

Your letterheads and envelopes should match in both colour and quality in order to present a professional image. If you use different coloured paper in order to differentiate different aspects of your initial booking package keep these to a minimum in order to avoid a messy or over-fussy look. Use pastel shades, not only are these easier to read text from but they will send out a much calmer message than a document which has been printed on a bright or neon colour background.

**Recycling stationery**

This should be avoided. Re-using old envelopes by sticking labels across them presents a poor professional image, as does amending letterheads or compliment slips by sticking on new address labels. Instead if you want to prove your 'green' credentials buy good quality recycled paper and envelopes from a reputable source.

**Labelling your products**

If you produce CDs or tapes, or your own brand of essential oil mixes, or any other products, make sure you also produce labels or insert details which clearly mark you out as the producer of these goods. Such items often get loaned out or given to friends, family or work colleagues – if your details are professionally displayed on these items, you may find yourself with another client.

# That all-important first contact

## Greeting clients

Ensure that your client feels welcomed and that any information they share with you will be treated in a confidential and respectful manner. Give your client time to settle themselves, hang up their coat or use the bathroom. Most clients appreciate some space at the beginning of a session in order to settle down, particularly if they have been rushing to see you straight from work and may be bringing with them the stress of their work or the journey. If you offer your client a drink as part of the settling-in process, make sure this is simply water unless you have time to allow your client to finish a hot drink.

### Recorded messages

Your answerphone should have an appropriate message recorded for your business callers. If you record this yourself any potential clients will be getting a feel for you as a person by listening to your message even if they can't speak to you direct. Ensure your message is friendly as well as professional.

### Fax machines

Some clients will find it more helpful to keep in contact with you by fax. If you use your fax machine to reply to any client queries you should ensure that your response is made on your business headed paper and that you include a confidentiality statement. A form of words is given below:

> The information in this fax is confidential to the intended recipient and may also be privileged. If you are not the intended recipient, please destroy this fax and notify the sender. You should not copy this fax or use it for any purpose, neither should you disclose or distribute its contents to any other person.

### Replying to emails

If you get enquiries by email, it helps to have some standard replies ready in order to speed up your responses to requests for further information. If you keep these in a word-processed format in a separate folder, you will be able to catalogue your replies and cut and paste these into your emails as appropriate.

It's good practice to include your signature and your contact details at the bottom of any emails you send, and you should also include a confidentiality statement. A form of words is given below:

> This email and any attachments which may be included are confidential to the intended recipient and may also be privileged. If you are not the intended recipient, please notify the sender and delete this email from your system. You should not copy it or use it for any purpose, neither should you disclose or distribute its contents to any other person.

### Your website

Your website may be the first point of contact for some of your clients, so make sure that you have a well-designed site which is regularly updated and conforms to the accessibility guidelines for websites.

**Compliance with DDA standards**

It is a requirement of the Disability Discrimination Act that all information provided by a service provider be accessible. This includes your website. There are a number of organisations which can offer advice and help you to design web pages that can be accessed by most users whatever the nature of their disability or impairment.

Whilst many people with sight problems have at least some useful vision and can read web pages in exactly the same way as a fully sighted person, the needs of others with poor sight can vary considerably. Some can read large text, while others can read only smaller letters. Some will require a strong contrast for the colour scheme. Because individual needs vary so much, your website will need to be flexible in design, allowing a user to utilise their own browser to adjust the text and colour settings to suit their own particular needs.

People with little or no vision read web pages with the help of access technology installed on their computer, either via synthesised speech software or Braille software. *If your site is poorly designed it could mean that a user utilising this equipment will not be able to access it.*

**The general advice from the RNIB on background, text and colours is:**

- Choose a single, solid colour for your background – avoid images, patterns or bright colours.

- The contrast between the background and the text is generally more important than the colours.

- Make sure that your colour scheme can be over-ridden by the user's browser settings.

- Avoid images of text, as these are graphics and will not be able to be overridden by the user's browser settings.

- Capitals should be avoided as many people find these difficult to read.

- Restrict the use of italics as these can also be difficult to read.

- Avoid underlining text, as this can be difficult for some people to read and can be confusing as it usually indicates a link.

- Moving, blinking or auto-refreshing text are all best avoided – not only are they hard to read but are inaccessible to anyone using speech or Braille output.

♦ Text size is not so much of a problem, medium size text is fine, but you should ensure that you use relative font sizes in your code rather than absolute, as some browsers can't override absolute font sizes.

For further information about web-based accessibility issues, see Chapter 12 which lists a number of useful websites and contacts where you can get further advice and download accessibility guidelines.

## Good housekeeping

There are a number of routines or practices which will help the smooth and efficient running of your practice and promote your professional image. **These are:**

♦ keeping good filing habits and file structures
♦ backing up your business systems
♦ keeping clients informed
♦ keeping the work environment clean and tidy and supplied
♦ knowing where and when to make referrals
♦ using encryption, passwords and screen savers.

### *What are your filing habits?*

Make sure you have a place in which to store everything you use, as this will help you get into the good habit of filing documents away as soon as you have finished using them and putting away any equipment after use. Files and other items left lying around not only make your practice look cluttered, they can be dangerous, cause a breach of confidentiality or cause you to waste time looking for documents.

Your filing system, whether manual or computer-based, should be simple and well-structured and you should allow yourself some time each day for keeping your filing system up to date. Any files or documents which are no longer current should be archived and kept in your long-term storage system, and any documents which you no longer need to keep, and which contain personal information, should be disposed of securely. For more information about keeping and disposing of records, see Chapter 6. You should also get into the good habit of regularly clearing down your phone messages, whether voice or text, and your emails.

## Backing up your computer files

It is good practice to keep your computer files and system regularly backed up. How frequently you need to do this will depend on how you use your computer system. Ideally any files you have been working on should be backed up the same day, with a regular back up of all your files at least once a week. Keep your floppy disks or CD copies of your files in a locked filing cabinet when not in use, and make sure that they are appropriately labelled.

## Keeping your clients informed

You should keep your clients informed of:-

◆ any changes to your practice details, such as a new telephone number
◆ any changes to your practice code of conduct
◆ any times when you will not be available
◆ any changes to your professional memberships
◆ any need to cancel or re-schedule appointments.

Any changes to your practice details should be updated as soon as possible on your website and on all your business stationery. You may also find it useful to include an appropriate message on your voicemail and answerphone and include the new details in any emails you send. Changes to your code of conduct could include changes to your cancellation policy or charges as well as any changes to your professional memberships, so it is important to regularly review this document to ensure that it is up to date.

*If you need to cancel or reschedule appointments for whatever reason, it is good business practice to let your clients know as soon as possible.* Contact your client by phone rather then email, as not everyone checks their emails every day. Keep your clients informed if you are going away on holiday or will be out of contact for any reason. Make sure you record a suitable message on your phone and leave a message on the auto-reply facility on your email system. If you would like to have your messages dealt with while you are away, investigate buying in some services. Some companies offer a PA/secretary service to handle all your business calls whenever you are unavailable, and you may find this useful.

## Using encryption, passwords and screen savers

It is important to keep all your computer-based information secure in order that any personal data you may be storing on your computer is kept confidential. Your system should be password protected, and your files should be encrypted. Encryption software will often be pre-installed or included in the software bundle you received when you bought your computer. If you don't have any encryption software you can download shareware software from the internet. For more information about encryption software, see Chapter 12.

It is good practice to have a screen saver which is password protected. Get into the habit of always leaving your screen saver on whenever you leave your computer for a few moments as this will avoid any potential problems with others trying to access your files.

### Keeping the work environment clean, tidy and supplied

Keeping your work environment clean and tidy is important for the maintenance of your professional image. *Whether you clean your rooms yourself or have a cleaner to do this for you, make sure that it is done regularly.* If you use towels, pillow cases, couch covers or any other linen as part of your work, make sure you have a routine in place for getting these items washed and returned to your practice on a regular basis, or check whether it is cost-effective to get a company to do this for you. You may also find it cheaper, easier or simply more hygienic to use some disposable items, such as paper cups or paper handtowels.

Keeping adequate stocks of everything you use is important, not only will it save you from the embarrassment of running out of anything, it could also save you money. If you maintain your stocks and supplies at a certain level you may be able to save money by ordering in bulk, and also save time by ordering any supplies just once a month.

### Making referrals

There are times when you will need to make a judgement as to whether you can, or want to, work with a client. This may be because you lack certain experience in relation to your client's problem, or your therapy is not appropriate for your client's needs, or you feel you have little rapport with the client which may hold back the healing process. *In these situations you will need to make a referral to someone else.* It is good practice to keep a list of other therapists or organisations to which you can refer your client. Make sure you keep telephone contact details as well as email or website details. Most clients are happy to accept a referral when you explain the reasons to them. It is more professional to refer someone on and your clients will often thank you for doing so.

# CHAPTER NINE

# Marketing Your Practice

> Effective marketing is as much about the subconscious messages you send out as the active role you take in presenting your practice.

## Why do I need to advertise?

Advertising is the way in which you communicate your business message to others. Unless you actively work at letting people know about your complementary health practice and the range of conditions and problems you can treat, you will not be able to build a successful client base.

**There are three main factors you should consider before doing any advertising:**

- the unique features of your practice
- the kind of people who would be interested in what you have to offer
- the media you are going to use for advertising.

## What's unique about my practice?

In order to attract new clients you need to present your practice in some way which differentiates it from the rest. When making an initial decision about which practice to contact, your clients will want to know why they should come to you for sessions rather than a similar practice in the next street, or the other practices listed next to yours in the trade directories.

Consider what unique selling points your practice has to offer. What can you promote about your practice that others don't mention or offer. **These could be things such as:**

- offering a free initial consultation
- offering home visits
- offering evening or weekend appointments
- promoting any new or specialised techniques you have been trained in
- listing any areas you specialise in and your qualifications for treating those conditions
- detailing your experience of and willingness to work with couples or groups
- detailing any other therapies you are trained in and how you integrate these into your work.

Make sure that these details are included in any leaflets you send out, and that they feature on your website and in any advertisements you make.

## Who would be interested in my work?

The kind of people who will be interested in your work will vary according to the therapy you offer. For example, if you are working as a massage therapist this will have a more general appeal than someone who is working as a cranio-sacral therapist, similarly a session with an aromatherapist is more likely to appeal to women than men. Take some time to review your therapy and the kind of person it might benefit. Start by making a list of the sort of things you help your clients to achieve – is it greater relaxation, a toned and supple body, pain relief, the resolution of personal problems?

Once you've listed the main benefits to be achieved from your work, you can then start to match these to personality types, particular occupations or other social groupings such as mothers with young children. *This will then help you to target those people who will have a genuine interest in what your practice has to offer*. For example, if your therapy is particularly helpful to those in high-stress jobs you might want to directly target groups such as teachers, corporate managers, firefighters, nurses and doctors.

## How should I advertise my practice?

There are many types of media that you can use. These include:

- local, national, trade and specialist newspapers, journals, directories and books
- posters
- advertising boards outside your practice
- the internet – your own website or using on-line health directories
- local radio
- leaflets
- notices in local newsagents' windows or cards in local supermarkets.

Some of these methods are more expensive than others, so it is worthwhile contacting your colleagues in the same line of business to find out what has worked well for them before you decide to part with any money.

## How much should I spend on advertising?

How much you spend on advertising is up to you – but it doesn't have to be a costly venture. There are many ways in which you can creatively market your practice for minimal cost.

As part of your business and financial planning process you should already be clear about the amount you have allocated for your advertising budget, at least for the first year. Don't be tempted to exceed it, but do be prepared to monitor how much income you have achieved from your various marketing approaches so that you can decide how this money can be better spent in subsequent years.

**Your advertising costs can be roughly divided into three categories:**

- advertising methods which cost you nothing
- advertising methods which cost a minimal amount
- advertising methods which are more expensive.

It's good marketing practice to use all three methods.

### Advertising methods which cost you nothing

There are a number of way in which you can market your practice for free. Single line entries in trade directories will often be free as will any listings on the trade directories' websites. As the paper-based directories are only published once a year you will need to check the deadline for publishing. If you have missed the deadline you can still usually be entered on the website and your details will automatically go in the paper-based directory when it is next published. It is important to get listed in the usual trade directories such as *Yellow Pages* or *Thomson* as this will often imply that your business is well-established.

As well as trade directories you can usually get your practice details entered for free on a number of complementary health websites, for further information see Chapter 12. You can also leave your business cards in the specially provided cardholders which are available in most large supermarkets – you will need to register your details with the supermarket first.

*Another very good way of increasing your client base is to offer to give a talk about your work, with possibly a short demonstration of your techniques, to local organisations or groups.* This allows people a chance to see the 'face' behind the therapy and gives you a chance to actively promote your therapy to an interested group for free – make sure you take along plenty of leaflets.

### Advertising methods which cost a minimal amount

There are also a number of advertising methods which will only cost you a relatively small amount of money to put into effect. **These are:**

- putting up posters
- distributing leaflets
- getting your own website
- putting notices in shop windows
- having your own advertisement board.

### Posters and leaflets

If you are thinking of putting up posters or distributing leaflets, you only have to meet the cost of the materials. An A4 poster, despite its small size, can still be quite eye-catching particularly if you use a good contrasting background colour. Many clubs, healthcare groups and sports venues will allow you to put up your poster for no charge. Distributing leaflets can be done in a variety of ways, none of which need cost you anything. For example, you could hand out your leaflets at tube or bus stations – make sure you're there at the times when people are commuting to or from work. You could also hand your leaflets out at the entrance to a major shopping area, or place them under the windscreen wipers of cars in the car park at your local supermarket.

## Websites

Getting your own website can be a very useful way of attracting in more clients, and it won't cost a lot to get a basic website up and running even if you require some expert help to set this up in the first place. The on-going costs are low, and once your site is established you can add whatever extra information you wish or even use the site as a 'shop' to sell some of the products you have developed. It is important that you have a web presence, so if your budget for advertising is tight, spending your budget on creating a website will more than repay its cost to you in your first year of trading. I know many therapists who get up to 40% of their clients through their websites – so it's worth investigating.

## Notices in shop windows

Many shopkeepers will allow you to put up a small notice or a poster in their shop windows for a small charge, and some will allow you to do this for free. If you are thinking of advertising in this way it's often more successful where you have some link with the shop or business, for example, having a poster in your hairdresser's window. Your hairdresser is likely to speak to their clients about your work, especially if they query the notice in the window. You may therefore find it helpful to offer your hairdresser a free treatment so that they can tell their clients just how good your sessions are.

## Your own advertising board

If your practice is situated in a local shopping area and you can get permission to have an advertisement board on the pavement outside your practice, you will probably earn back the cost of the board in the very first week you set it up. It can work even more effectively for you if you can attach some leaflet holders to the board so that any passers-by can pick up a leaflet to find out more about your practice without the need to call in. Make sure you get a board where you can easily change the information you display, as this will increase the interest in your practice.

## *Advertising methods which are more expensive*

Other advertising methods can be more expensive, such as advertising in newspapers, magazines and books, or advertising on local radio. If you choose to advertise in this way you are likely to have to spend in excess of £300–£500. A credit card-sized advertisement in a trade directory such as *Yellow Pages* is likely to pay for itself. Similar sized advertisements in books, magazines or newspapers are more of a risk unless you can time your advertisement to coincide with a review of your particular type of therapy or an article on a health problem which lists your therapy as one which has positive benefits for sufferers of that condition. Radio ads are also risky in terms of recouping the money you have spent on them. A better way would be getting the opportunity to be interviewed for local radio, which will give you a chance to showcase your practice and help some callers on-line. The radio station will normally announce your contact details on air and will also give these out to any callers.

### Keeping track of your expenditure on advertising

Whatever methods you use to market your practice, you should keep a running total of just how much each method is earning you. You can either set this up on a spreadsheet or create a manual log. This log should be reviewed at the end of the financial year, in order that you can make some judgements regarding your advertising practices. Keep a note of all your forms of advertising, even the 'free' ones, and assess each method against the cost of that method and the percentage of your total income it has generated for you. This way you will quickly be able to see where you should put both your money and your effort.

## What approaches should I take?

**There are seven main approaches which you can use to promote your therapy practice:**

- direct marketing
- personal selling
- public relations
- the internet
- word of mouth referrals
- promotions
- consolidating your image.

### Direct marketing

This means that you are positioning your advertising so that it is relevant to a particular group of people, such as teachers. This form of marketing succeeds if you have thoroughly researched your target group's needs and requirements and you can prove that your therapy has a number of benefits for this group, for example, it helps them to relax or helps with their personal time management or long-term plans.

You will need to personalise the information you send out to these groups, so make sure that you include information which is relevant to their needs. Don't send out copies of your more general practice brochure unless you accompany this with additional group-specific information. It will help your marketing if you can give some testimonials, or cite direct examples of how your therapy has helped such people and be able to list the particular skills and experience you have to offer.

**Direct marketing can include the following:**

- mailshots
- door-to-door leaflet drops
- leaflets inserted in local newspapers or magazines
- phoning groups or organisations.

**Mailshots**

There are companies which will organise this for you, but if you want to keep your costs down you can do this yourself. Once you have decided on the groups you are going to target and the information which you are going to send out, scan the local trade directories for their listings of suitable businesses or schools, or whatever your target group is. Then all you need to do is print sufficient copies of your letters and leaflets and send them out.

*It is often a good idea to ring round a couple of your target organisations before doing your mailshot* in order to find out the title of the person who usually deals with this kind of correspondence, for example in a school it may be the office manager rather than the headteacher. This ensures that your mailshot is more likely to be dealt with sympathetically rather than disposed of the moment it arrives. Include a brief request in your covering letter that your leaflets be placed on the staff noticeboard if there is no one who can make immediate use of the information.

It is also a good idea to send all your letters to a particular group on the same day.

**Door-to-door leaflet drops**

This is something which you can have as an on-going activity. Keep a supply of your leaflets ready for those 'quiet' moments we all experience from time to time, and use that spare time to drop some leaflets off. You can use this method for targeting anyone in your local area. *Although the take-up rate is likely to be no better than 1%, it is a very cheap way of marketing your practice.*

Do keep a note of which streets you have targeted, so that you can work a new area each time. The best time to do any door-to-door drops is on Sunday afternoons, as your leaflet will not get mixed up with any other post and people generally have more time to spare and therefore the chances of your leaflet getting read are greater. Make sure your leaflet stands out in some way, for example use coloured paper (but not fluorescent shades) and have an eye-catching message on the front of your leaflet that makes the reader want to learn more.

**Leaflets inserted in local newspapers or magazines**

If you are thinking of advertising in this way, you will need to carefully select the type of magazine that your leaflet is going in to ensure that it contains information which is related to your therapy, such as a health magazine – or that its readership is likely to be interested in your practice, for example a business magazine where you are advertising your life-coaching practice. For local newspapers it is often more helpful to target this to coincide with specific local events such as a local health fair or mind-body-spirit type event. *Other ways in which you can use the local newspaper for targeting a particular group is when certain health awareness days or weeks are on,* such as the national day for stopping smoking, or breast cancer awareness week.

**Phoning groups or organisations:**

Advertising in this way gives you a chance to directly answer any questions that the group or organisation might have about your particular therapy and how it could help their members. It may be from this that you are invited to give a talk, or are invited to work some sessions for a couple of hours each week, or they may even agree to circulate your details to all their members – so be flexible in your thinking and the ways in which you can work with the organisation. *The more personalised you can make your approach the better.*

*Personal selling*

This is the method a lot of big businesses use when they employ people, such as a salesperson, specially to talk to targeted companies and groups on a face-to-face basis. This is a very effective method for big business, so if you take this idea and think creatively about your own distinctly smaller business, how can you put this into operation? Well, there are couple of ways. If you substitute yourself for the salesman, then one of the most logical first moves would be to target a group of people you think could benefit from your help and support and offer to give a free talk about your work. *Personal contact really does help to sell a product, and if you have a problem with the thought of selling yourself, just remember that you are effectively 'selling' health benefits, and what could be better than that?*

Even handing out leaflets about your practice at a shopping centre or train station can involve you in some personal contact and a chance to 'sell' your practice. As you give out the leaflets you could ask the individual whether they would like to have some further information about the practice, introduce yourself and be prepared to answer any questions. And remember, that although that individual may not require your help, a member of their family or a friend or work colleague might – you've got the 'floor' so take full advantage of it. Most people are impressed when you make a personal approach, as it implies that you are sufficiently interested in them to give them some of your time and attention.

> **Don't forget to carry some leaflets and business cards with you wherever you go – remember, anyone and everyone you speak to is a potential client.**

## Public relations

This can be a very useful way to make people aware of your practice. It is also a good way of building up a network of useful contacts. Giving a talk or a demonstration for a local organisation, or at a club event, can really help to build your reputation.

If you want to take this further you could try to get a local newspaper or local radio to include an interview with you. One way of attracting some press coverage is to offer your services for free for a particular reason. This could be teaching some relaxation exercises to smokers who want to give up smoking on the national 'stop smoking' day, or offering to teach basic baby massage techniques to new mothers at a newly set up local children's centre. To succeed with getting the coverage you require, you will need to make sure that your event can provide 'interest' – for example, there are always smokers looking for ways to help them quit smoking, that you have a 'hook' – such as running your event on the national day, that there is a 'need' which you are meeting – for example, smokers who are trying to quit are often tense, and that there are some 'benefits' – such as mothers learning massage skills to help relax and bond with their new babies. *Any press coverage you get will be free and will imply a degree of credibility and endorsement of your practice.*

### The internet

Getting your own website gives you a brilliant chance to promote your business. **You can use it for:**

◆ explaining in detail how you work
◆ providing the client with further information about their problem or medical condition
◆ providing links to other organisations or even articles the client may find of interest
◆ selling any of your own products
◆ demonstrating your work in action eg videoclips, recordings etc.

It is one of the cheapest and most versatile methods of advertising your practice, and it can grow and develop as your business expands. Make sure that whoever develops your website does so in accordance with the accessibility requirements of the Disability Discrimination Act. For further information on the accessibility guidelines, see Chapter 8 and Chapter 12.

### Word of mouth referrals

These can be one of the best and most powerful ways of getting your business promoted. A personal recommendation is an easy way to gain new clients. If you are only just setting up your practice it can take quite a while for this to work for you, but eventually you may be getting up to 40% of your new clients by this means. In the meantime you could ask every satisfied client for a testimonial or a few short statements about their experience or sessions. This will 'seed' the thought for your client to recommend you to others – if they haven't already done so.

*You achieve this growth by your own good work, effective practice management, looking after your clients and always seeking to develop your own skills so that your sessions are as effective as possible.*

### Promotions

You can offer promotional prices on any of your products which you sell, in order to increase your sales and to encourage new clients to buy your products. Even if you are not selling any products, you can use promotional advertising in other ways. For example, offer a free initial consultation or, depending on the therapy you work in, you could also offer a reduction in your fees for any clients booking a block of sessions, or offer a discount to certain groups such as students or elderly people.

*Any promotion will add value to your services, or products, and will usually encourage new clients into your practice.*

### What image should I be conveying?

The image and message that your practice conveys is a very important part of your marketing, albeit subconscious. It can make or break your credibility. You should consider every aspect of your practice from the perspective of the subconscious messages it sends to existing and prospective clients. **For example:**

◆ Do you have a 'brand' that clients will recognise?
◆ How clean, tidy and comfortable is your working area?
◆ Do you have a colour scheme or logo that is easily recognised?
◆ Does your business stationery conform in respect of colours, font, style and quality?
◆ Will you or any colleagues who work with you wear uniforms?
◆ Do your clients know how to find and contact you?
◆ What name have you given your business?

> **When you think about your practice's image you should really be thinking about how you wish to be known and remembered by your clients.**

For more information on how you can set a good image by paying careful attention to detail, see Chapter 8.

# CHAPTER TEN

# Future Plans

## The next five years begin now

It may seem very strange to be thinking or planning quite so far into the future when you have just started putting all your efforts into a new business. But if you truly want your business to succeed you should already be looking to the future with some tentative plans of your own that you want to work towards. So allow yourself to dream a little and indulge in some creative thinking. If you could wave a magic wand and make your wishes come true, what would they be for your practice in five years' time?

> If you have a clear 'blueprint' of how you want your future to be, you are sending out the right signals to your mind and body to work harmoniously to achieve this future. You can only achieve that which you can create in your mind – and yes, creative visualisations do work.

## Why it's important to plan

A practical plan for the future growth and direction of your practice is essential. If you have formulated a business plan you have set up your own personal blueprint of what you want to achieve and the very fact of putting this on paper will clarify your thinking, help you set realistic objectives and allow you to monitor and adjust your progress as necessary.

## Planning for success

The key to success for your practice is to evaluate:

- where you are going
- why you want to go there

- what objectives you want to achieve
- when you want to achieve your objectives
- how you are going to achieve your objectives
- whose advice or support you might need in order to achieve your objectives.

### Where are you going?

In order to answer this question you need to consider your long-term vision and ask yourself what the main aim of your business is – what is your ultimate goal? Once you are clear about this everything else you do will be directed towards achieving this. Your long-term vision will reflect your goals for the next three to five years and it can be strategic rather than financial. For example:

> *I want to be able to offer the best possible assistance to anyone seeking an alternative to drug-based pain relief.*

Now you have your vision statement it should remain fairly fixed. This now gives you the opportunity to start working on the various elements necessary to achieving that vision.

### Why do you want to go there?

You may know that you want to be able to offer effective non-drug pain relief, but now you need to examine why. What are your motives for wanting to achieve this vision? **These could include:**

- a wish to specialise
- a particular interest in that topic
- some personal reasons.

If you have a particular interest in pain relief, and it is an area that the therapy work you are engaged in is known to have some positive influence on, you can take this further and explore the idea of specialising in this subject. Your personal motivation and commitment to achieving any vision statement needs to be high, but if you find that whenever you talk about your subject to other therapists, clients or friends you start to get a 'buzzy' feeling, and others comment on how you get 'carried away', the chances are that you are already highly motivated.

A personal reason for achieving a vision can also be a very strong drive. It may be that you yourself have a condition which requires regular pain relief and have found your techniques to be wholly beneficial for your own purposes and now wish to share these with others. Or it could be that you have a close family member or friend who has benefitted from your work to date but still needs some more help – hence your wish to research this further to be able to *offer the best possible assistance.*

### What objectives do you need to achieve?

These are the short-term goals which you need to achieve in order to attain your vision statement. They will need to be reviewed regularly and updated, in order that you remain on course to achieving your long-term goals. Spend some time breaking your vision down into its component objectives. **These could be short-term goals such as:**

◆ to complete a review of the current literature on this subject
◆ to search the internet for any research on this topic, on-going or otherwise
◆ to investigate what expertise is available
◆ to ask for volunteers for testing new techniques
◆ to update my research methodology and statistical techniques
◆ to find a person who can 'supervise' me during this work.

This is not an exhaustive list. Once you have set your vision statement you need to allow yourself time to brainstorm all the necessary steps you will need to take to achieve your long-term goal.

### Assessing your objectives

Both your vision statement and your shorter-term objectives need to have a 'reality' check to see if they are SMART. **SMART objectives are:**

◆ specific
◆ measurable
◆ achievable
◆ realistic
◆ timed.

Now you have this means of assessing your objectives – put it into action. Go back and check each of your objectives in turn against these criteria. For example, if you now wish to assess your original vision statement:

*I want to be able to offer the best possible assistance to anyone seeking an alternative to drug-based pain relief*

how does this measure up?

### Is it specific?

Yes. Had the statement been worded differently, such as –

*I want to be able to offer assistance to anyone seeking pain relief*

you could have met your vision by simply offering paracetamol to anyone who presented in pain, or taking them to the nearest chemists. Now you're looking more critically at this statement is there anything you would like to change? Do you really mean *anyone* seeking non-drug pain relief, or do you want to qualify this further because the people you really want to work with are those seeking non-drug pain relief for chronic pain problems? If so, amend your vision statement.

*I want to be able to offer the best possible assistance to anyone seeking an alternative to drug-based pain relief for a chronic pain problem.*

### Is it measurable?

How will you be able to measure that yours is *the best possible assistance*? If there is no other research to draw on you will need to set your own criteria and determine what this part of the statement means. How would you decide that your treatment plan overall was successful? You may decide that it means:

*over 70% of people treated achieve a reduction in their pain measurement rating of more than 40%.*

This then becomes your qualifying statement by which you measure your success.

### Is it achieveable?

In the example given, you won't know until you've completed all your research and testing whether your qualifying statement is achieveable, and you will therefore need to revisit and evaluate that statement as your plans progress. However, a quick review of the current research literature will help you to assess the results other therapists are currently achieving so that you can adjust your statement accordingly.

**Is it realistic?**

To assess whether your vision is realistic, you should look to yourself and your own skills Do you have the necessary skills and resources to achieve this goal? **Can you answer 'yes' to the following questions?:**

♦ Does your therapy work help people with chronic pain to reduce their pain levels?
♦ Are you already having some successes in your work?
♦ Are you committed to undertaking further research?
♦ Do you have the time available for this research?
♦ Do you have the financial resources available for this research?
♦ Do you have the necessary equipment and environment for this research?

If so, you can go onto the next stage of assessment. If your answer to any of these questions was 'no', you will have to look for some creative solutions and make whatever adjustments are necessary to achieve a 'yes' response.

**Is it timed?**

No. But it would be useful to include a timescale. Setting timescales and deadlines will help you to focus on your objectives and schedule your time more effectively. When do you want to achieve your vision, three or five years from now? Amend your vision statement accordingly.

*I want to be able to offer the best possible assistance to anyone seeking an alternative to drug-based pain relief for a chronic pain problem – and to achieve these skills by July 2007.*

## Reviewing your objectives

You will need to carry out this exercise for all your objectives from your vision statement down to your short-term goals. Make any changes that are necessary and then quickly assess any objectives which you have changed through the SMART assessment procedure again. Get into the habit of doing this every time you make a change as it will help you to keep full control over the planning and change process.

## When do you want to achieve your objectives?

Setting a timescale for each of your objectives as well as your overall vision will help you piece together your plans. Once you have decided on a target date for achieving your vision statement, go back and look at each of your objectives and prioritise them accordingly. How long will each one take to achieve and which ones can you work on at the same time?

> Setting a target date for your vision is vitally important – it will help to keep you on course by giving you a clear focus for your work.

### How you are going to achieve your objectives?

In order to achieve your vision, you will need to have achieved all the objectives you have detailed as being an integral part of the process. This will cause you to break each objective down into further steps or mini-objectives. One of the objectives listed earlier was

*to investigate what expertise is available.*

**How you are going to achieve this might be by:**

- conducting an internet search for related articles and documents and noting authors
- contacting the authors
- contacting any training establishments mentioned in the literature
- sending out a request for further information to a related egroup
- using your supervisor/mentor's expertise.

Each of these tasks or mini-objectives will need to be noted and have time allocated for the task. Sometimes in order to achieve an objective you may require further training, or a new piece of equipment, to travel or raise some extra funds. By this continual breaking down of each action into its required tasks, you will be able to plan more effectively for the resources you require.

### Whose advice or support do you need?

It is unlikely that you will be able to achieve your vision in isolation. **You may require:**

- other colleagues to work alongside you testing techniques on volunteers
- peer group members to test various techniques on each other and quantify the results

- the support of an appropriately experienced person to act as your supervisor/mentor
- to buy in certain expertise
- someone to act as your administrator.

Each of these individuals will need to be approached at the appropriate time, so this adds another level to your planning process.

## Planning decision 'tree'

The following decision 'tree' on page 161 (Figure 19) outlines the thinking you need to apply at each stage to test your vision statement and to assess your objectives in order that you can identify the individual tasks you will need to accomplish.

## Scheduling your plan

Now that you have set your objectives and identified the individual tasks you need to carry out in order to achieve your vision statement, you should start scheduling time for this work. Either make or buy some year planners (undated are best), and gather together felt tip pens and coloured stickers. Use the different colours and stickers to highlight the various tasks in 'gantt' chart fashion – see example below.

| Jan | Feb | Mar | Apr | May | Jun | Jul | Aug | Sep | Oct | Nov | Dec |
|-----|-----|-----|-----|-----|-----|-----|-----|-----|-----|-----|-----|
|  | search web for articles and author |  |  |  |  |  |  |  |  |  |  |
|  |  |  |  | get in touch with author |  |  |  |  |  |  |  |

Start by putting in your target date for achieving your vision statement – big bright sticker! Then start allocating time slots to the short-term objective and tasks.

Once you have completed allocating tasks and objectives to your year planner, the last stage is to incorporate this schedule into your financial plans, costing activities and equipment purchases as necessary. And when you've done all that you should be well on the way to accomplishing your vision.

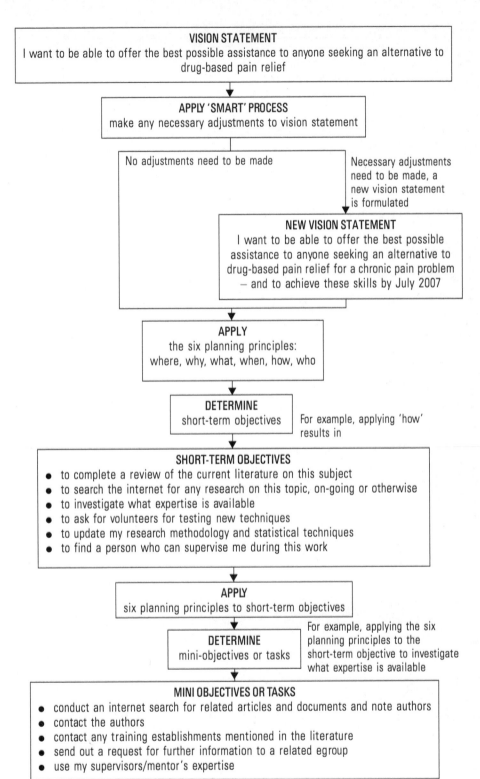

Figure 19. Planning decision 'tree'.

## Creative thinking to remove blocks

At any stage of the planning process, whether it is formulating your vision statement or assessing how to achieve one of your major objectives, you may experience some 'blocks' regarding your thinking processes. For some people their creativity just flows, others find it harder to let their imagination go. **If you are finding it difficult to get any useful ideas you might want to try:**

♦ brainstorming with others from your peer group
♦ exploring some of the ideas that other colleagues are working on
♦ taking some time out to review your motivations and personal skills base
♦ talking over your fledgling ideas with someone who can help to shape your thinking
♦ attending a creative or lateral thinking course
♦ meditating or taking a short holiday to clear your mind.

It's quite often people input that helps clear the blocks. Even talking about a problem to someone else can trigger off a series of new and more creative ways of approaching or dealing with the issue. For more information about creative or lateral thinking courses, see Chapter 12.

# CHAPTER ELEVEN

# Looking After Yourself

> *'I shall consider my own well-being to be important*
> *And I shall endeavour to be true to myself'*
>
> *(taken from the Healer's Promise – NFSH)*

## Why is this important?

As a therapist you, more than most people, should be aware of the need for balance in your life and the importance of looking after yourself. Some training courses for complementary therapists encourage their students to check their PEMS state each day. **PEMS stands for:**

- physical
- emotional
- mental
- spiritual.

Monitoring these states on a daily basis and recognising you own needs and requirements seems a good starting point. In order to do our work well, and to get the most satisfaction out of life, we need to be in good health. This means that we need to recognise our own limits, become aware of own vulnerability and actively seek to restore the balance by whatever means necessary.

## Keeping home and work life separate

Whether you have a family to look after, or live on your own or with a partner, it is essential that you keep your work life from intruding on the rest of your life. This can be hard to achieve when you are first setting up and there are all kinds of inducements to make you take your work home, or to work very long hours.

**To get some order back into your life try the following:**

◆ physically separate your work from your home life
◆ do not take work home
◆ have set days and times when you are working
◆ keep your business phones separate from your home phones.

## How can I physically separate my work and home life?

This is easiest if your practice is located outside the home. *However, even if you are working from home you can keep the two separate.* If you have a room set aside as your therapy room and do not need to use it for any other purpose, make sure you shut and lock the door at the end of your working day and resist any temptation to go back in and do any pre-work on some of your cases. If your therapy room is also a family room, then make sure you lock away all your files, put your phone onto answerphone and shut down the computer – just as you would if you were working from an office. It can also help if you rearrange the furniture, symbolically changing the layout to 'family' use.

> **Keeping your work and home life separate is all about setting boundaries. Whether these are physical, mental or emotional they need to be real and everyone, including yourself, needs to respect them.**

### Leaving work at 'work'

Whatever your working arrangements are, get into the good mental health practice of leaving your work behind when you have finished for the day. This practice can be made easier if you get into the habit of literally, or symbolically, locking your work away. If your practice is a mobile practice, have a filing cabinet or lockable cupboard at home where everything, and I mean everything, is stored away after use. *Don't take any business calls, or respond to any faxes or emails outside of your working hours.* You may also find it helpful to have ten to 15 minutes of quiet time between finishing work and going 'home' in order to sit, still your mind, maybe meditate for a while or listen to some music to help you unwind. This can become your ritual for closing down after work each day and it may help you to keep the boundaries distinct.

### Boundary setting

Boundary setting can also involve setting new rules for your friends and family members. Whether or not you work from home, you are likely to get some friends, or members of your family, who believe it's alright to phone you while you are at 'work' or ask you to deal with some personal requests during your working day. This is generally because you're no longer seen to be 'employed' in the usual sense. *You need to be just as tough with friends and family as you would be with clients trying to contact you out of hours.* Persistence pays. If you don't take their phone calls or deal with their other requests, they will eventually be re-educated to your new work boundaries.

### Setting your working times

Trying to keep your work and home life separate can be made a lot easier if you set the days of the week you are going to work, and the times. This way you are clear about what constitutes your working day, your clients soon fit into your work pattern and your friends and family will know when they can get in touch. This will also allow you to plan your free time so that you can maintain your social life.

## Monitoring your workload

If you haven't already set yourself a regular work pattern by allocating the days and times when you are at work, the chances are that you may be exceeding the hours you wish to work in a week. **To bring your workload back under control you need to:**

◆ keep a record of all your work activities for a week
◆ take a note of the total time you spent on each activity
◆ total up the time which you spent in leisure activities
◆ review your income for the week.

Once you have carried out these activities it will become clear just how much time you spend working; what the work entails; whether you managed to get any free time and just how much working this way earned you in a week.

On reflection, was this a balanced week? Did you keep to your work hours? What did you learn about your work activities – are there some activities that take up a disproportionate amount of your time? If you didn't manage to get any leisure time, why was that? Was it due to family or work pressures? And for the number of hours that you worked that week, do you think you were adequately paid? *If any of these questions is giving you pause for thought, you should investigate the matter further to see what you can change, drop, increase or delegate.*

## Time management

We should all of us have plenty of time for the things we need to do, but so many of us waste it in unnecessary actions. If personal time management has always been a problem for you, you are going to need to learn some new ways of working. **Some classic time wasting activities are:**

- never letting the phone go onto answerphone
- reading and responding to your emails several times a day
- not replying to your correspondence as soon as you have read it
- trying to find a document which you haven't filed away
- constantly shifting items or documents because there's no place to store them
- living in a state of clutter
- starting an activity but not finishing it because something else distracted you.

Do you recognise yourself in any of these? If so, you have a time management problem.

If you can use your time effectively you will be able to get more work done, and if you can get more work done you will potentially earn more; and if you can get more work done you will not have any need to take work home to finish it and will therefore have more free time to spend doing whatever you please. *All that is needed is some personal re-education in order to bring some balance back into your life.*

When you are busy working let the phone go onto voicemail, you can always pick your messages up later. If you keep interrupting what you are working on to answer the phone, you will lose your concentration and it will take an extra few minutes for you to effectively get back to your work. If you truly value your work, give it the time and attention it deserves in order that you can complete it and move on.

### The 'one-touch' principle

As a general rule, doing the same activity more than once in a day (if you don't have to) is a waste of precious time, as is handling anything more than once. So get into the good habit of only reading and responding to your emails and your mail once a day. Make sure you have time to complete these tasks, if you're not sure how long this will take then leave this activity to a point in the day when you know you will have more time. Anything you can't manage to complete in one sitting will need to be dealt with the next working day. Following through on the time management principle of handling a document only once means that as soon as you have completed your correspondence, file it. This will save you wasting time searching for any documents which you left lying around and now can't locate.

The 'one touch' principle can also be extended to the movement of furniture or pieces of equipment. Make sure everything you use in your work has a place where it gets stored away. If you haven't got sufficient or suitable storage then make a decision to get some and discipline yourself to use it. This will also help you to get rid of any clutter, which generally tends to accumulate if your storage space is inadequate or difficult to access. If your workspace is cluttered then you will be in a constant loop of moving things around in order to work and wasting time in the process.

For further information about time management, see Chapter 12.

## Looking after your own health and safety

As you are going to be responsible for your own health and safety at work, make sure that your working area is always kept clean and tidy, that there are no cables trailing across the floor which you or your clients could trip over, and that your room is adequately lit, ventilated and heated. Also, ensure that your equipment is fit for purpose and make sure you get any repairs or replacements carried out before things become hazardous.

### *Siting and using your computer equipment*

**Remember to follow the computer user guidelines and:**

♦ locate your computer at right angles to any natural light source
♦ use a screen filter if you suffer glare on the screen from overhead lights
♦ use a desk lamp if the other lighting in the room is unsuitable
♦ adjust your monitor until it is at the correct working level to avoid neck and back strain
♦ use a wrist rest
♦ don't work for longer than two hours without taking a break
♦ make sure that the room is adequately ventilated.

When you are working at the computer make sure you are sitting at the right height. Get a chair which you can adjust to suit your needs and make sure it has castors. **The general guidelines for the correct seating position are:**

♦ your foot/calf, calf/thigh, thigh/back and forearm/shoulder angles should be at 90° to each other
♦ the bottom part of your spine (the lumbar vertebrae) should be in contact with the seat back
♦ your knees should almost touch the front edge of the seat
♦ your forearms should be able to rest, or be supported, on a level with the keyboard.

If, once you've adjusted the height of your chair your feet don't fully touch the ground, invest in an adjustable footrest so that your feet and legs are in the most appropriate position while you work. Make sure you are sitting straight whilst working. If you find that you are constantly turning your head in order to work from a book or notes, get a book-rest or paper-stand so that the documents are held closer to your working eye level and thereby minimise the potential strain on your back and neck.

If you aren't a touch typist – now would be a good time to learn. Free tutorials are often given away with software packages, so try out the software which came with your computer. Also, discipline yourself to use the keyboard shortcuts wherever possible, rather than the mouse, as it is becoming accepted that excessive mouse use is one of the main contributors to RSI (repetitive strain) type injuries.

## Holidays and time out

To prevent 'burn out' or illness, you need to make time for yourself. Schedule some holidays or long weekends in your diary at the beginning of the year. You may not keep to the dates but it will serve as a reminder to take some time off. If you have children at school, make sure you take some time off during their holidays and this will help you to get into a good routine of regular time off. You could also try working to a six or seven week pattern – allowing yourself to take a long weekend or even a week off at the end of the six weeks' working period. It's a practice that has worked well for me. If you take regular breaks it's often easier to keep up with a full working week and a busy practice, so don't regard it as an indulgence but more of a necessity.

> **Make sure you take a full two weeks holiday at some point in the year – and cut yourself off from work completely.**

As well as more formalised time out, don't neglect your body clock in other ways. If you find yourself flagging after a hectic morning and have some free time after lunch, take a nap. You don't need to sleep for long, so set your alarm to make sure that you wake up in plenty of time for the next client. If you regularly find that you want to droop around lunchtime, listen to what your body is telling you. It may be you should adjust your working day to reflect this personal 'down-time' and allow a nap to become a regular habit. Many therapists change their hours in order to work at the times in the day when they feel more energised.

*Therapy work can be one of the most draining and stressful occupations to be in. If you are constantly working with people whose personal energy is low you need to make sure that you have routines in place to re-energise yourself and protect your own energy levels.*

## Supervision and mentoring

Undergoing personal supervision, or working with a mentor, can help you to offload and deal with any client problems which otherwise might be weighing you down. Your supervisor will usually be a more experienced therapist working in the same treatment areas as yourself and will therefore be best placed to advise you on maintaining your boundaries, taking time out, any further training which may help you to cope more easily with certain aspects of your work and may also work with you in a therapeutic capacity if that is appropriate.

If you don't already have a supervisor or mentor, get in touch with your training school to see what recommendations they can make. For further information about supervision and mentoring, see Chapter 7.

## Personal development

The more well-rounded and balanced you are as an individual, the better your work will be, the more you will enjoy it and the happier you will be in all areas of your life. In order to achieve this balance you need to 'think outside the box'. Are there any skills you've always wanted to learn or develop which could help to you achieve a greater balance in your life? Or are there any places which you've always wanted to visit? Any burning desires that you were prevented from achieving? *Think creatively.* Wherever you've felt a lack of something in your life relates to a potential imbalance.

If you've always longed to take singing lessons – why don't you? After all, not only could this help you to develop and find your own authentic voice, it could also be a means of letting go of some of your emotional issues. Although it may seem somewhat indulgent, fulfilling any 'lack' in your life could have a positive effect on your work. If you are now learning to project your voice with ease, you will be able to teach or lecture more effectively because you have taken the strain off your voice.

> **Everything you learn and every experience you have can enrich both your personal life and work life – if you stay focused on the positives of that experience and allow your creativity to flow, nothing will ever be wasted.**

# CHAPTER TWELVE

# Further Help

## Access to health records

The Access to Health Records Act 1990 gives individuals certain rights of access to their health records. Much of the earlier legislation regarding the individual's rights to see their records has now been subsumed within the Data Protection Act (see *Data Protection Act*). You can view or purchase a copy of this Act on-line, contact:

The Stationery Office
Website:        www.hmso.gov.uk/acts/acts1990/Ukpga_19900023_en_1.htm
Telephone:      0870 600 5522
Email:          customer.services@tso.co.uk

## Accessibility issues

For the legal requirements regarding accessibility, see *Disability Discrimination Act*.

For details of organisations offering guidelines and advice on accessibility issues related to website design, see *Websites – accessibility issues*.

## Advertising on health-based websites

The following websites allow you to list your details for free and usually allow you to enclose a short summary of the therapies you practise, any specialities you may have developed, and the conditions you frequently treat. You can also post up any requests for information on their news and noticeboard sites, and advertise any courses, workshops or seminars that you may be holding.

HealthyPages Complementary Health and Healing Directory
Website:          www.healthypages.net

Positive Health magazine
Website:          www.positivehealth.com

## Advice

You can get free advice on a wide range of topics through the on-line advice service operated by Citizens Advice. This can range from such diverse topics as how to get your company name registered to advice on pensions and National Insurance contributions. Whilst this service does not offer the full detail of the information which is held by individual Citizens Advice Bureaux, it can help you work through some of your issues and will provide further contact details for more information. Contact:

Citizens Advice
Website:          www.adviceguide.org.uk

## Benefits

If your income drops below a certain level, depending on the number and ages of the people in your household you may entitled to financial help. The following benefits may apply:

Housing Benefit and Council Tax Benefit: for more information about these benefits contact your local authority.

Working Tax Credit and Child Tax Credit: for more information about these benefits and contact details see *Tax credits.*

## BUPA

BUPA is a private health care company. Complementary therapists used to be able to work as part of this scheme if registered with BUPA. The policy now appears to have changed and anyone wishing to work with BUPA will need to have an orthodox medical background. If you would like further information, contact:

BUPA
BUPA House
15–19 Bloomsbury Way
London WC1A 2BA

Telephone:         0800 00 10 10
Website:          www.bupa.co.uk

## Business Link

Business Link can offer you free advice on setting up your business and details of any government grants or schemes which may be available in your local area. For further information contact:

Telephone:         0845 600 9006
Website:          www.businesslink.org

## Children Act

The Children Act 1989 established the concept of parental responsibility. You can view or purchase a copy of this Act on-line, contact:

The Stationery Office
Website:           www.hmso.gov.uk/acts/acts1989/Ukpga_19890041_en_1.htm
Telephone:         0870 600 5522
Email:           customer.services@tso.co.uk

## Companies House

Companies House can advise you on the legalities of setting up and naming your company. You can download copies of their guidance booklets from their website. Contact:

Companies House
Crown Way
Cardiff
CF4 3UZ
Telephone:          (029) 2038 8588
Website:             www.companies-house.gov.uk

## Complementary health directories and magazines

The following on-line directories and magazines advertise complementary health training courses, business opportunities, health products. Contact:

HealthyPages Complementary Health and Healing Directory
Website:             www.healthypages.net

New Health magazine
Website:             new-health.biz/courses/course1.htm

Positive Health magazine
Website:             www.positivehealth.com

## Creative and lateral thinking

Edward de Bono has written a number of books on lateral and creative thinking. He also runs training courses in these skills. I've listed my favourite book below – it should help you overcome any blocks regarding your business plans:

*Six Thinking Hats*, Edward de Bono (Penguin).

Illumine Training runs training courses in lateral thinking and creativity, some of which are directly related to improving your business. Contact:

Illumine Ltd
Argyll House
3 Shirley Avenue
Windsor
Berkshire SL4 5LH
Telephone:      (01753) 866633
Website:        www.illumine.co.uk

## Credit card transactions

One of the simplest and cheapest ways to accept payments by credit card is to set up an on-line account with a company such as PayPal. PayPal allows any business or consumer with an email address to securely send and receive payments online. PayPal's service lets users send payments for free, and it can be used from PCs or web-enabled mobile phones. A percentage is charged on every transfer made to you (0.7% – 2.9%).

You can use this service to 'invoice' a client by simply entering the client's email address and the amount you are requesting. The client gets an email and instructions on how to pay you using PayPal. You can send and receive money in a number of currencies. For more information contact:

PayPal
Website:        www.paypal.com

## Data Protection Act 1998

If you would like further information about this Act, or to check whether you need to register, contact:

Data Protection Act
Website:             www.dataprotection.gov.uk

The website contains a handy on-line questionnaire which will guide you through assessing whether you need to register and, if so, will help you to complete the notification on-line. You will then need to print off a copy and send the form to the address listed below. If you don't want to complete the form on-line, you can ask for the notification form to be sent to you by completing the request for a notification form which can be found on the home page. You can also phone the notification help line, they will send you a draft notification form based on the information you will be asked to provide over the phone.

Information Commissioner
Wycliffe House
Water Lane
Wilmslow
Cheshire SK9 5AF
Telephone:           (01625) 545740 (notification help line)
Fax:                 (01625) 524510

A notification handbook and self-assessment guide can be accessed at:
Website:             www.dpr.gov.uk/notify/1.html

## Disability Discrimination Act 1995

If you would like further information about the provisions of this Act, log on to:

Disability Discrimination Act
Website:             www.disability.gov.uk

Disability Discrimination Act – N. Ireland
Website:             www.dhssni/gov.uk

A copy of the Code of Practice can be viewed at:
Website:             www.disability.gov.uk/dda

For further help contact the DDA helpline:

Telephone: (0345) 622 633
Faxback service: (0345) 622 611
Textphone: (0345) 622 644

## Ebooks and publishing

There are a number of companies specialising in producing and publishing ebooks. You will need to check out what is on offer in terms of contracts, costs, print runs etc. The following is one of the larger sites which you might want to compare. You can download an information pack on producing your ebook, and also use the company to publish your ebook:

Authors OnLine
Website: www.authorsonline.co.uk

## Egroups

An egroup is one of the easiest ways for a group of people, such as therapists, to communicate on the internet. To set up an egroup you will need to register with Yahoo! or a similar service provider. It doesn't cost anything to set up an egroup. For more details, contact:

Yahoo!
Website: www.yahoo.com

## Encryption shareware

Any personal data held on your computer should be encrypted for confidentiality and security reasons. The following company offers downloadable encryption shareware:

VersionTracker
Website:          www.versiontracker.com


## Health and Safety Executive

The Health and Safety Executive offers a national general enquiry service. It can be contacted at:

Infoline:          08701 545500
Fax:               (02920) 859260
Email:             hseinformationservices@natbrit.com
Website:           www.hse.gov.uk


## Independent financial advisers

If you want to find an independent financial adviser in your area, contact:

Find an IFA
Website:           www.unbiased.co.uk


## Marketing

For more ideas on marketing you might want to get a copy of the following book which focuses on low-cost ideas for the complementary therapist:

Steven A. Harold, *Marketing for Complementary Therapists – 101 tried and tested ways to attract clients* (How To Books) ISBN 1-85703-806-1.

## Medical charities

Charity Choice is an encyclopaedia of charities on the internet. Contact:

Charity Choice
Website:        www.charitychoice.co.uk

## National Insurance (NI) contributions

For more information on NI contributions contact the Inland Revenue:

Inland Revenue
National Insurance Contributions Office
Benton Park View
Newcastle upon Tyne NE98 1ZZ
Telephone:       (0191) 213 5000
Website:        inlandrevenue.gov.uk/nic/

## NHS provider number

You will need an NHS provider number if a GP refers a patient to you and the GP is applying for the cost of that patient's treatment to be met by the local health authority. Having an NHS provider number does not confer any endorsement of your skills or qualifications, as there is no formal process in the application procedure for your qualifications or competence to be examined. It is purely a code to identify you as a person who contracts in the NHS internal market. To apply for an NHS provider number, contact:

ISD4A
380D Skipton House
80 London Road
Elephant and Castle

London SE1 6LH

| | |
|---|---|
| Telephone: | (020) 7972 6049 |
| Fax: | (020) 7972 6538 |
| Email: | ocsmail@doh.gsi.gov.uk |

## Office furniture and equipment

### IKEA – business

For business furniture and equipment – they have some very stylish and space saving ideas. You need to have a business bank account if you want to open a business account with IKEA. You can fax your orders and they will deliver the goods. Contact:

IKEA

| | |
|---|---|
| Telephone: | 0845 355 5662 |

### Viking

For business stationery, furniture and equipment – same day delivery in certain areas. You don't need to have a business bank account to open an account with Viking. Very reliable service. Contact:

Viking

| | |
|---|---|
| Freephone: | 0800 424444 |
| Freefax: | 0800 622211 |
| Website: | www.viking-direct.co.uk |

## Office stationery

### Viking

For business stationery – same day delivery in certain areas. You don't need to have a business bank account to open an account with Viking. Very reliable service. Contact:

Viking

Freephone:        0800 424444

Freefax:          0800 622211

Website:          www.viking-direct.co.uk

## PayPal

See *Credit card transactions*.

## Pensions

To get the facts you need to start planning your future, you can download or order a free introductory guide to pension options from the government's impartial pensions information site. Contact:

Pension guide

Telephone:        0845 7313233

Typetalk:         0845 604 0210

Website:          www.pensionguide.gov.uk

Pension guide

Freepost

Bristol BS38 7WA

## Performing Right Society

This society licences anyone who uses music in their practice. The money from the licence fees it collects is then distributed to its members – the writers and publishers of music. The current annual licence fees are:

for using radio in an area containing up to 19 seats – £57.32

for using a CD player in an area containing up to nine seats – £57.32

For further information, or to purchase a licence contact:

Performing Right Society

| | |
|---|---|
| Telephone: | 0800 68 48 28 |
| Fax: | (0173) 331 2712 |
| Email: | musiclicence@prs.co.uk |
| Website: | www.prs.co.uk |

## Prince's Trust

The Prince's Trust offers financial help and support to young people aged 18–30 who are setting up in business. For further information contact:

The Prince's Youth Business Trust
18 Park Square East
London NW1 4LH

| | |
|---|---|
| Website: | www.princes-trust.org.uk |
| Freephone: | 0800 842 842 |
| Fax: | (020) 7543 1200 |
| Textphone: | (020) 7543 1374 |

In Scotland, the Prince's Trust is known as the Prince's Scottish Youth Business Trust, and offers support to young people aged 18–25. For further information contact:

The Prince's Scottish Youth Business Trust
6th Floor
Mercantile Chambers
53 Bothwell Street
Glasgow G2 6TS

| | |
|---|---|
| Telephone: | (0141) 248 4999 |
| Email: | firststep@psybt.org.uk |
| Website: | www.psybt.org.uk |

## Royalty free music

Royalty-free music is music which you pay a one-off fee to use, and which doesn't then require a licence. The copyright remains with the producer of the music but you are free to use the music in your work. The following site allows you to download royalty free music, and it includes a variety of music such as easy listening and New Age.

Website:         www.royaltyfreemusic.com

## Self-assessment tax form

You can complete your self-assessment tax form on-line. Contact:

Inland Revenue:     www.inlandrevenue.gov.uk/sa/

## Self-employed – registration

You must register as self-employed within three months of the date when you first started self-employment. To register, contact:

Inland Revenue
Telephone:       08459 15 45 15
Textphone:       08459 15 32 96
Website:         www.inlandrevenue.gov.uk/startingup/register.htm
Website:         www.inlandrevenue.gov.uk/pdfs/pse1.htm

## Taxation

The Inland Revenue has a very user-friendly site which should be able to answer most of your questions regarding your tax situation. They also operate a small businesses helpline where you can speak to advisers direct about any tax queries you may have. There are links from the main site to other sites that may be of interest, such as Child Tax Credit and Working Tax Credit.

Inland Revenue
Website:               www.inlandrevenue.gov.uk

## Tax credits

You don't need to have children to qualify for tax credits, as these benefits are income related. Child Tax Credit and Working Tax Credit are part of the government's programme for alleviating poverty and making work pay. For more information or to claim on-line, contact:

Inland Revenue
Website:               www.taxcredits.inlandrevenue.gov.uk/Home.aspx

## Time management

There are any number of books written on this topic, but you might like to try the following:

Kenneth Blanchard and Spencer Johnson, *One Minute Manager* (Harper Collins).
Mark Forster, *Get Everything Done and Still Have Time to Play.*

## Training courses

As well as looking at the training course advertisements listed in the relevant professional journals and magazines, you could try the following complementary health directories and on-line magazines:

*HealthyPages Complementary Health and Healing Directory*

Website:                    www.healthypages.net

*New Health* magazine
Website:                    new-health.biz/courses/course1.htm

*Positive Health* magazine
Website:                    www.positivehealth.com

## Websites – accessibility issues

The following are some useful contacts which can help you by providing guidelines and advice on how to make your website more accessible for those clients who are visually impaired. For advice on good design, contact:

RNIB
Website:                    www.rnib.org.uk
Email:                      seeitright@rnib.org.uk

AbilityNet
Website:                    www.abilitynet.org.uk
Email:                      enquiries@abilitynet.org.uk

For downloadable accessibility guidelines, contact:

AccessIt
Website:                    www.accessit.nda.ie/guidelineindex_1.html

## Writing a book

There are numerous books written on this topic, but a good place to start would be to review the following:

Nancy Smith, *501 Writers' Questions Answered – A comprehensive guide to writing and getting published* (Piatkus). ISBN 0-7499-1512-9.

*Writers' and Artists' Year Book*. Published annually by A & C Black.

There are also some useful magazines which detail common problems and how to overcome them, and list useful contacts and ways of getting your work published. These are just a few, and you should be able to get copies from any large newsagents or stationers:

*Writing Magazine* and *Writers' News* – published by Writers' News Ltd

Website:            www.writersnews.co.uk

*Writers' Forum* – published by Writers International Ltd

Website:            www.writers-forum.com

# Index